Transforming Your Life through Self-Care

Transforming Your Life through Self-Care

A Guide to Tapping into Your Deep Beauty and Inner Worth

Carolyn A. Brent

ROWMAN & LITTLEFIELD
Lanham • Boulder • New York • London

Published by Rowman & Littlefield
An imprint of The Rowman & Littlefield Publishing Group, Inc.
4501 Forbes Boulevard, Suite 200, Lanham, Maryland 20706
www.rowman.com

6 Tinworth Street, London SE11 5AL, United Kingdom

British Library Cataloguing in Publication Information Available

Library of Congress Cataloging-in-Publication Data

Names: Brent, Carolyn A., author.
Title: Transforming your life through self-care : a guide to tapping into your deep beauty and inner worth / Carolyn A. Brent.
Description: Lanham, MD : Rowman & Littlefield Publishers, [2019] | Includes bibliographical references and index.
Identifiers: LCCN 2018051748 (print) | LCCN 2019003002 (ebook) | ISBN 9781538120859 (electronic) | ISBN 9781538120842 (cloth : alk. paper)
Subjects: LCSH: Self-actualization (Psychology) | Self-care, Health.
Classification: LCC BF637.S4 (ebook) | LCC BF637.S4 B7334 2019 (print) | DDC 158.1—dc23
LC record available at https://lccn.loc.gov/2018051748

∞™ The paper used in this publication meets the minimum requirements of American National Standard for Information Sciences—Permanence of Paper for Printed Library Materials, ANSI/NISO Z39.48-1992.

Printed in the United States of America

To my dad, Pastor William L. Brent, ThD: I will be forever grateful to have been blessed with him, the most wonderful and amazing parent I could have ever hoped or asked for. His words of wisdom: "No excuses. Find a way. Believe for a miracle. Press on till you win. *Don't quit!*"

Contents

viii   *Contents*

Acknowledgments

$\mathcal{M}$any individuals deserve to be acknowledged for the support they have given me in life and in the preparation of this book. A special thank you to the most exhilarating people in the world whose contributions have broadened my worldview: International Federation of Bodybuilding and Fitness (IFBB) professionals; national thought leaders in the pharmaceutical, science, and political arenas; Dave Ramsey, financial genius; Dr. Wayne Dyer, self-development and spiritual growth leader; and Kathy Palokoff, author, educator, and chief igniter.

I'd like to extend my gratitude to the following professionals who have contributed to my health, wellness, and financial lifestyle journey: Dr. Delia Weiss; Dr. John Webster, orthopedic surgeon; Dr. Perry Bard, chiropractor; Jessa Carter, PA-C; Dr. Nathan Hare, Dr. Oscar Jackson; Dr. Sean Feezell; Dr. Kirsten Fleischmann; and financial professionals Duane Thompson, Kevin A. Guttman, and Gregg Nevills.

A special thanks to the men and women who shared their personal stories or were interviewed for the purposes of this book: Lashai Ben Salmi, Thell Dodd, John Sandifer, Jose Flores, David Octavio Gandell, Beatriz Osorno, Christine Jackson, Ben Courson, Angela James Maness, Zulieth Mendoza-Gayle, Anthony Parrinello, Goldine Eismann, Annthia Phan, Neil Koppel, and Maria Kramer.

Special recognition to my family: Thell Dodd, John Sandifer, and my extended family from Ghana; and my God-sister Philomena Brew whom I've never met in person; God-son Martin Brew, daughter-in-law Sara, and granddaughters Josephine and Martina. I have been blessed to have them by my side for many years. They have always offered an illuminating perspective on several subjects covered on these pages. Our lengthy conversations have sparked several ideas and challenged many assumptions. For that, I will forever be grateful.

My sincerest thanks go to those who helped me prepare, package, and promote this book: Suzanne Staszak-Silva, Elaine McGarraugh, Jen Huppert, Leticia Gomez, Kathy Palokoff, and the editorial team whose contributions have helped make the writing and the production of this book a reality.

A big thank you to the people behind the scenes, who helped me during my journey to transform my life through self-care by tapping into my deep beauty and inner worth: Val Jaentschke, NPC master of ceremonies; Jocelyn Jean, IFBB Pro bodybuilding champion and bodybuilding coach at FitRx; NPC Dayana Cadeau Classic 2016; Andres Miller, IFBB & NPC Promoter; Carla Dunlap-Kaan, American female body-building champion; Sandi Jackson, life fitness/wellness coach; David and Shaun Nunes, coaches and consultants at Nunes Pro Fitness; Dr. Josefina Monasterio, life coach, weight-loss expert, and female body-building champion; Jeff Jansz, eighty-three-year-old kickboxing and personal trainer; Ernestine Shepherd, American body builder who is best known for being, at one point, the oldest competitive female body builder in the world; Patricia Valenti, IFBB Pro; Roody Exantus, IFBB Pro; Rhonda Spicer, women's body builder and personal trainer; Mel Peters, makeup artist; Lysia's Hair Studio; Annthia Phan, Lush Beauty Bar; Jesse Stein, Stein-O-Mite Media; Mel Peter's Photography; NPC news online http://npcnewsonline.com; Grandpa's Dream Productions; Andrew Mondia, Jim T. Chong, and Pastor Johnny White; Carol Staab, anchor/reporter, and Roni Lewis, cohost on *NTV's Good Life*, in Nebraska; Cheryl Miller, cohost, Bill Bevins, former cohost, Greg McQuade, host, Jessica Noll, executive producer, and Torri Strickland, producer, on *Virginia This Morning*, WTVR CBS 6; Janelle Wang, anchor, KNTV; Dr. Brenda Wade, author and national TV personality; Margaret Larson, former anchor and reporter at KING 5; Janice Edwards, host and producer, *Bay Area Vista*; Perry Atkinson, president, the Dove TV; Jacqueline Hayward Wilson, former anchor, WUSA 9; Cynthia Butler, former producer, ABC News, *Sacramento & Company*; and Mary Nicholson, president for Healings In Motion.

Introduction

$\mathscr{I}$ have spent a long time thinking about the right title for this book. Words are important. They can inspire or deflate. Ignite or extinguish. Drive you to action or move you to despair.

The words others use against us have power. But the words we use against ourselves are infinitely more powerful: "I am not worth it." "I can't." "I give up." We have all used those words against ourselves at some point in our life, and the results can be devastating.

On the flip side, words of joy and confidence help us achieve our dreams: "I am beautiful inside and out." "I love myself." "I am so worth it."

How do I know this? I know because of my own journey and talking to literally thousands of people who are searching for the answers and actions to age with grace, health, and wisdom.

I have physical ailments that could keep me in a life of pain and disability. I have left a spouse who betrayed our marriage vows. I have uprooted my life to move to a place where I literally knew no one. I have weathered the storm of family disputes.

But because of discipline and determination, I have taken the actions required to reclaim my physical, emotional, relationship, mental, financial, and spiritual health. At sixty-one years of age, I am thriving. I have tapped into my deep beauty and inner worth.

So let me start by carefully defining the key words in the title of this book: ***Transforming** Your Life through **Self-Care:** A **Guide** to Tapping into Your **Deep Beauty and Inner Worth***.

TRANSFORMING

Every day I read the courageous stories of people who have overcome incredible obstacles and tragedies in their lives. Every day I also read the stories of people using every excuse in the book to justify their actions and faults. I have come to the conclusion that the difference between these two groups of people is how much they are committed to transforming their lives.

Transforming occurs in two primary stages. The first is the aha moment when you recognize the need to change. The second stage is when you act with discipline and persistence.

We all have aha moments. You know the moment when it hits you.

Maybe it is the straw that breaks the camel's back. I have a friend who was married to a guy with a drug habit. For years they did the dance of him relapsing and her forgiving. One day she came home to find that he had sold her vacuum cleaner for some crack. She loved that particular vacuum cleaner. At that moment, her whole attitude toward him changed, and she got off the hopeless hamster wheel of thinking she could change him. She found herself and started living her life. Who knew a vacuum cleaner could inspire an aha moment?

Many of us have that aha moment when it comes to our weight. We see a picture of ourselves and feel embarrassed. We find out that we are suffering serious health consequences from our overindulgence in food and underindulgence in exercise. We get that wake-up call and immediately go on a diet and commit to exercising every day.

In both of these examples, you see action. Unfortunately, action requires ongoing discipline and persistence to be truly transforming. Even after my friend had her aha moment and acted, there were times she slipped back into old habits of how she interacted with her husband. And there is probably not a person reading this book who has not put back on the weight he or she worked so hard to lose.

True transformation requires the structure and control that makes you repeatedly do what needs to be done to achieve your goals—no matter if they are personal or professional. You see this bottomless discipline in world-class athletes like those in the Olympics. No matter what, they train and sacrifice because they want to be the best in the world. If they fall, they get up. If they are distracted, they refocus. They do what needs to be done every single day.

I also have witnessed this discipline in my ongoing work with caregivers. They structure their days so they can provide care to loved ones. They are intensely clear on their priorities and how they allocate their time and resources. They engage a support network to keep them motivated. Again, they do what it takes every day.

SELF-CARE

Self-care is simply caring for yourself no matter what the cost. It is about putting yourself first. I'm not talking about being selfish. What I am talking about is understanding that you cannot care for others unless you care for yourself. It's just like love. You cannot love someone else truly unless you love yourself.

Self-care is loving yourself. It is saying that you are important and then following through with consistent action.

When I see people fail at diets or exercise programs, I hear many excuses. "I don't have the time." "It's not going fast enough." "My kids need me." "I don't have money." "It's boring." The excuses are countless, and what is really hard to understand is that the people making these excuses really believe they are true. They do not see them as rationalization for not doing things they committed to. And ironically, often these people are highly disciplined in other areas of their lives. They run businesses. They run households. They are financially stable. But self-care is elusive. And because of that, they will never quite achieve their goals and feel fulfilled.

Self-care requires self-control. This is not just my opinion. Research backs me up. A 2013 study by psychologist Wilhelm Hofmann and his team of researchers at the University of Chicago showed that people with high self-control are happier than those without it. These people spent less time debating whether to indulge in behaviors detrimental to their health and are able to make positive decisions more easily.[1]

GUIDE

This book is your guide. And I am your guide. I take this responsibility very seriously. I know the effect my own guides (or coaches) have had on my life. I want to have the same effect on yours as you transform your life through self-care.

There are two things you need to know and to take very seriously. First, a guide is just a guide. You can look at a map or read a travel guide while lounging on your couch. But if you want the adventure of seeing another country and experiencing other cultures, you have to get off your butt and actually get in the car, plane, or train. The same is true for transformation.

I can only guide you. You must do the work.

Second, each of us is a unique individual. What is in this book worked for me and has worked for countless others. But it is not a prescription for success. You need to make it your own. And the first step is knowing what is safe and healthy for your own body and mind. That means you should consult with your trusted team of health professionals before you embark on any dietary or exercise changes in your life.

DEEP BEAUTY AND INNER WORTH

I have often been told that I am a beautiful woman. As a body builder, I have cultivated a shape that makes people amazed and, sometimes, envious. I take pride in my looks and work hard to make the most of my God-given attributes. And it is always fun when people try to guess my age. I've never once had someone hit the right number.

But what I know completely is that beauty truly is only skin-deep. Deep beauty comes from a heart, soul, mind, and body that are joyous, grateful, and generous. It comes from truly enjoying life on a cellular level. It comes from working hard to be the absolute best you can be and then sharing that experience with others. It is about knowing your inner worth.

We all have deep beauty and we intuitively recognize people who have tapped into their inner worth to find happiness. We are drawn to them not only because of what is on the outside but also from the glow that seems to originate inside. There is a wisdom, peace, and charisma that shine forth from people who have accessed their deep beauty. We might see this beauty in a ninety-year-old great-grandmother or an eight-year-old child.

Tapping into this deep beauty is essential. And the beauty of it is that it is attainable by all of us.

HOW TO READ THIS BOOK

This book is designed to be read from top to bottom or by selecting chapters that particularly resonate with you. I do strongly recommend that you start reading each chapter from the beginning of the book, which will help "Wake Up Your Deep Beauty," since it forms the basis for my recommendations throughout the book and is at the core of my own personal transformation. Understanding the concepts outlined in the beginning will truly help you have more successful and sustainable outcomes.

I have also included many stories in this book. All of them are real, but I have changed the names of the persons involved. What is important is their story and not who they are.

As you read this book, you'll see I have included questions at the end of each chapter to help you tap into your deep beauty and inner worth. These are probing questions that will help you access a part of you that is necessary to transforming your life through self-care.

As you answer these questions, I strongly recommend that you record your answers. Writing them down will do two things: First, it will make your words more powerful and concrete. Second, it will provide a record of your journey as you transform your life.

Some people like to write in a journal. The act of putting pen to paper can have profound effects. Numerous studies indicate that journaling can provide health benefits to individuals. Other people like to use their computer to capture their thoughts. I personally create binders for myself and my clients, where we can include not only our own answers to questions but also articles, cartoons, and even drawings that may help us on our journey.

Whatever way you choose to record your answers is fine. What's important is that you use the power of your deep beauty and inner worth to make the changes that will lead you to a healthier and happier life.

Becoming the Authority of Your Life

 *O*ver the past ten years, I have been working tirelessly to reclaim authority over my mental, emotional, and physical health. The road I've traveled has been a long one as I transformed my life through self-care.

It started with an important first step. I became the authority of my life.

What do I mean by this? You have probably figured out by now that I like clarity in language. It puts us on the same page so we can work together to achieve goals. So let's take a look at the word "authority."

The word has two meanings. The first is to be an expert on something, as in "She is an authority on eighteenth-century quilting techniques" or "He is an authority on the music of Bruce Springsteen." Usually being an authority relates to a specific skill or knowledge set.

Can you imagine anything more important than becoming an authority *on your own life?* To understand what makes your body feel best or how to find a serene place when you are agitated? To have thoughtful knowledge of your past and present so you can move forward into the future? To know what you need to keep yourself healthy mentally, physically, emotionally, and spiritually? What could possibly be more deserving of your efforts?

The other meaning of "authority" is the power to command thought, opinion, or behavior, as in "the president has authority in the United States" or "my mom was the authority in our home." This definition is equally relevant to transforming your life through self-care, because it means that you have the power to command your thoughts and behavior. You can act on what you think and what you do.

You can take back your power—your authority—from things and people you have given it away to. You may have given away that power to a bad relationship or job. You may have given it away to doctors, without questioning and learning about your own body. You may have given it away to satisfying your cravings for foods and drink that have been harmful to you.

Here's the good news: Even if you have given away your authority and let other people and situations become the expert on you, you can get that authority back. Even if you have let others command your thoughts and behavior, you can get that authority back.

Becoming an authority on your life is an ongoing process. You learn, make mistakes, recalibrate, and keep going. But it starts with acknowledging your role—that you are the authority, not anyone else.

THE FORMULA FOR BECOMING AN AUTHORITY

While on my self-care journey, I discovered an important formula that I would like to share with you:

Fierce Determination + Laser-Focused Actions + Bottomless Discipline
= Deep Beauty + Inner Worth

There's nothing more powerful than having a made-up mind and then going for your goal every single day with intensely focused actions and bottomless discipline. It will give you the knowledge and confidence required to be an authority on your life. And this formula will allow you to not only tap into your deep beauty and inner worth but also replenish it.

Here's an important thing I want you to keep in mind right now and as you move into your new future: You cannot let the well of your deep beauty and inner worth dry up. By understanding that you are the source of your deep beauty and inner worth, and then constantly taking action to keep that well filled with clean, fresh, and life-giving substance, you will transform your life permanently.

That is what I now experience in my life and what I have helped thousands of other people achieve. I will be sharing aspects of the formula throughout this book, but let me demonstrate some of those aspects by sharing some of my own journey with you.

WHEN DREAMS COME CRASHING DOWN

From 1996 to 2003, I was healthy and living the most opulent life I'd ever dreamed of living. I was thriving in my career as a clinical education manager working with medical researchers and key opinion/thought leaders across the country in the pharmaceutical industry. I had education, a high six-figure income, and career status. I had achieved the American Dream.

That changed dramatically in 2000 when my hero and best friend—my dad—was diagnosed with dementia. In order to care for him, I got off my career path and stepped down from my clinical education manager position to become a sales representative because it required significantly less travel.

Three years later, a seemingly innocuous incident happened that once again changed my life. I arrived at a storage facility to count my monthly inventory, which was one of my job responsibilities. I began moving products around to organize my unit and decided to remove my shoes and put on flip-flops to get more comfortable. Ten minutes later, I tripped over a small box, stubbing my baby toe. Although I was in some pain, I didn't think much about it. We are talking one stubbed toe, right?

To my surprise, the bottom of my right foot turned completely purple. A few X-rays later, I got the bad news. I had shattered my fifth metatarsal bone, which is the long bone along the outer edge of the foot. My foot and leg needed to be cast immediately, and the orthopedic surgeon told me to stay off my feet for several months.

I stared directly into the doctor's eyes in disbelief and thought, "Nope, I can't afford to take off work for several months. I'll just have to work with a cast on." During that time, my dad was living in a private assisted living facility, and I was responsible for paying his hefty rent of $6,500 each month. I had no choice but to keep on working. I figured my foot would eventually heal.

Then nine months later, the next blow came. On September 19, 2007, my dad had a massive hematoma, bleeding on the brain. While I was dealing with the agony of seeing my dad's health take such a rapid turn, my identical twin sister and other siblings decided they wanted to take over his care. They had never taken any time to help in all of the twelve years that I was his caregiver.

I wish they had acted out of concern for my dad and me. They did not. When family members think there is money to be had, you may find yourself taking out restraining orders and spending time in probate court. That's exactly what happened to me. I was served with restraining orders in three different county probate courthouses. At each court hearing, as we stood before the Judge, the plaintiff would drop all charges she had filed against me.

With the legal battles and everything that was happening, I had no time to process or recover. I was angry, depressed, and in astonishing physical and emotional pain. My life was spiraling out of control. The months of treating my body poorly and not taking time off work had resulted in a new set of physical ailments. I started having severe lower back pain. Sitting or standing for long periods caused my lower extremities to swell. My orthopedic surgeon warned me that if I did not start taking care of myself, I would end up in a wheelchair.

Then came the final blow: My beloved dad died. A distant relative notified me two weeks after his internment. My siblings did not even tell me that he had passed or where he was buried. Can you imagine the devastation, shock, and excruciating emotional pain I experienced?

One evening while I was home alone, my heart started beating so fast that I thought I was having a heart attack. I drove myself to a nearby hospital emergency room. After doing an EKG and other heart evaluations, the ER doctor informed me that I had experienced a panic attack.

At that moment, I knew I had to do something different to save my life. I had to take back the authority over my mental, emotional, and physical health. That's when I became my *own* caregiver, recognizing I had no other choice but to take action with laser-focused discipline and fierce determination on every level.

Mentally, I knew I had a tremendous amount of hard work ahead of me. And I understood that it was going to be a gradual, step-by-step process. I took ownership of my health and knew it was my responsibility. No one else could do it but me. I was the authority of my own life

THE POWER OF DETERMINATION

My story is dramatic, but not unique. Nobody walks through life unscathed. What do you do when you are facing devastating and unexpected life-changing events? Or when you are dealing with adult sibling rivalry and a loved one gets ill and passes? Or when you become the person with debilitating health issues? Or when the career you loved no longer exists?

To be honest, at my lowest point I was ready to give up. But I heard my dad's voice and knew I had to channel my love and passion for what he stood for back into my own life. I had to use my made-up mind as a major force in my life.

I started imagining the courageous healthy woman I used to be. I knew once I had my thoughts and actions in alignment, I would never allow a damn thing to ever stand in the way of the God-given authority of the person I was born to be.

Now I was ready to step out of my pity-party zone to be healthy again. I had fierce determination to never allow fear, naysayers, negative thoughts, stinking-thinking people, or devastation hold me back again. I had the faith to believe in me again.

PUTTING A PLAN INTO LASER-FOCUSED ACTION

First, I began working with a psychologist who helped me understand what I had been through and how to recover. I started journaling to get a complete understanding of my past in order to move forward to a brand-new beginning. Because of my newfound clarity and healing, I found my passion and honored it. I wanted to make a difference by helping other families to avoid having to experience the same pain I had gone through.

I started to focus on creating change in the current laws with the aim of protecting law-abiding caregivers. I discovered that there were no books on the market on the subject of adult sibling rivalry in connection with the end of life of a parent.

So I wrote the first book on the subject: *Why Wait? The Baby Boomers' Guide to Preparing Emotionally, Financially and Legally for a Parent's Death.* A subsequent book, *The Caregiver's Companion: Caring for Your Loved One Medically, Financially and Emotionally While Caring for Yourself,* is on the shelves of leading libraries, medical centers, and universities throughout the world.

Second, I focused on my physical body. I was committed to learning how to manage my chronic pain without becoming dependent on opioids or other pharmaceutical drugs. I began researching sports medicine doctors with specific expertise in kinesiology, exercise physiology, and sports psychology theory. I also studied fitness development for athletic performance, treatments, and sports nutrition.

I started working around my injuries by integrating the therapeutic and preventive use of exercise. Then I took it to the next level and began training as a body builder. I won first place in the Age 60 category and became a National Physique Committee (NPC) Masters Women's Figure Champion.

Finally, I focused on the body, mind, and spirit connection. I discovered a wellness institute with credentialed, trained professionals to help me master self-healing. I learned how to meditate mindfully. I began practicing daily the power of transmutation, an act that shifts anger to forgiveness and physical pain to physical wellness.

BECOMING AN AUTHORITY
THROUGH BOTTOMLESS DISCIPLINE

When I looked around at people I admired in life, I realized they all shared a common trait: bottomless discipline. Record-shattering athletes, leading businesspeople, and inspiring people in the arts exhibited discipline that made each of them an authority.

If I was to be the leading authority on Carolyn Brent, I knew I had to also act with bottomless discipline. What did that mean exactly? It meant going to the gym even when I didn't want to—which was often. It meant limiting how much I went out to restaurants because I could not control the food in the way I needed to keep my body feeling healthy. It meant practicing discipline every day about my spending habits so that I could live a life without the stress of unpaid bills. It meant surrounding myself only with positive relationships that nourished my soul, even when I longed for the passion of a lover.

It meant doing these things every single day, even when I did not want to, by reaching into the bottomless store of discipline I knew I had that was nourished by my deep beauty and inner worth.

If you are a mom or dad, what wouldn't you do for your children? You would starve so they had food in their mouths. Moms and dads do that every day around the world. If you were a child, what wouldn't you do for your aging parents? You would do what I did and joyously make sacrifices to give them the life they deserve. And if you were a best friend, spouse, or partner, what wouldn't you do for the person you love if that person was ill or in need?

You would practice endless discipline to make it right. That's what I want you to do now, because you are your own true love—nothing more and nothing less.

Now it's time to answer one of the questions I hear most from people around the world: "Where do I start?"

The place to start is to swap out your old thinking for new thinking. Start out by having a made-up mind and take back your birthright with authority and power. Just pause and ponder for a moment and think about the word "power." Are you willing to do what is necessary to have the authority over your life and health? Do you realize you are your only competition? No matter what your family health history, you still have the power to do your part. You have the power to take action regardless of your circumstances or age.

Here's the good news: Once you get serious about your health and get started, your body will start craving healthy nutritious foods and a good sweaty workout. Your mind will begin desiring additional inspirational and spiritual stimulation. And you will actively seek an emotional state where less drama and more peace feel exactly right.

"BECOMING THE AUTHORITY
OF YOUR LIFE" QUESTIONS

This is what I would like you to do right now: Go find a binder and carry it with you everywhere you go. Sit down for the next hour or so, write down the answers to the following questions, and list daily, weekly, monthly, and yearly goals.

1. What are your biggest obstacles to becoming the authority of your life?
2. What are your personal health goals, and how do you plan to achieve them? Do you trust your heart and believe that you will be successful?
3. Have you made the commitment to empower your life? Make a list of your commitments and sign it.
4. Are you willing to make discipline a top priority in your life? What actions have you taken toward becoming more disciplined? Name them.
5. Have you scheduled an appointment with a healthcare professional regarding your overall health? List what your results are.
6. Are you dealing with any emotional or stressful situations that you need to address? If so, have you contacted a healthcare professional to help you? What is your plan of action?
7. List each aspect of the plan.
8. What's your passion? Have you found it on your journey yet?
9. Do you need to ban any old habits, people, places, or things from your life? List them and tell why you need to ban them.
10. Have you identified what's been holding you back from becoming a healthier you? List whatever aspects apply, and write down how you plan to address them.
11. What educational resources do you need from specialized professionals?
12. What actions have you taken to master your thoughts with positive inspirational thinking?
13. Do you usually get a good night's sleep? How? If you do not, what's keeping you up at night?
14. What actions have you taken to connect your body, mind, and spirit?

· 2 ·

Why Partners, Family, and Friends Can Be Hazardous to Your Health

The people we love and respect the most have a significant influence on the major decisions we make in our lives. They encourage us and are there for us during both the fabulous and the hard times. We all hope to experience the power of this type of love, support, and respect over a lifetime.

But what if you are experiencing the total opposite, with signs of emotional, financial, or physical abuse? The consequences can be devastating and hazardous to your health. People who are themselves hazardous to our health can become major obstacles to our ability to become authorities on our lives.

In this chapter, I would like to show you how the power of love, self-care, letting go of fear, and the significant act of forgiveness can become your inner strength and enable you to tap into your deep beauty and inner worth. Let me start by sharing my own story.

A SAD BUT TOO COMMON STORY

In the summer of 2006, my dear friend Tony encouraged me to start having a little fun. He knew that the stress of caring for my dad, my job, and my physical ailments was having a toll on me. He suggested using the online dating site where he met the woman of his dreams. I decided to give it a try.

Almost immediately, I started receiving tons of connections. However, there was one attention-grabbing message that stood out from a man named Liam. For the next several months, we talked long-distance for hours by telephone. He was a great listener and so supportive. To top it off, he was smart, charming, and appeared handsome in his photographs. I thought, "Boy, I have hit the jackpot."

14

On a frosty cold Christmas Eve day at the San Francisco International Airport, Liam and I finally met in person for the very first time. I felt like I could hardly breathe as I laid eyes on this tall, broad-shouldered, dark, handsome, and charming man. I felt voltage rush through every vein of my entire body. Yes, we had great chemistry. It was love or lust for both of us at first sight. That was the beginning of our long-distance love affair, traveling back and forth from Florida to California for the next seven years.

When my dad died, I knew I needed a change from the memories that triggered so much sadness. In November, I joined Liam and his family for the Thanksgiving holiday in Florida. After a five-day romantic rendezvous, we both recognized we wanted to spend the rest of our lives together.

This is what he told me: "Carolyn, I want to protect, care, and provide for you. If we are going to do this right, you need to live in Florida." Wow, that was music to my ears. Though Florida was never on my bucket list of places to live, I thought, "How often do you find love?"

Once I returned to California, I hired a real estate management company to rent my home. Then I scheduled a moving company to move all of my earthly possessions across the country. I was looking forward to being with the man I had fallen in love with.

After settling in a new state, home, and life, we got married. Although we were newlyweds, I spent a significant amount of time home alone due to Liam's hectic work schedule. At that time, I became laser-focused on achieving optimum health by practicing deep meditation, body building, and writing. I felt blessed. And I thanked God for my new life with my partner/friend.

Within a year, Liam's time away from home became more intense and stressful. I started feeling isolated, ignored, and excluded. Then I started facing the truth that Liam's behavior toward me had changed. He was not giving me back the love I was giving to him. I realized we had actually spent more time together when we lived apart.

Over time, things changed even more. When Liam was home, he started treating me as if I was his servant, acting irrational and going into sudden rages over the slightest little things. He began to complain about my clothes and my body, which he thought was too thin.

I thought, "Where is this nonsense coming from?" As I started recognizing the emotional and verbal abuse creeping in our relationship, I also began to wonder if Liam was having an affair. When I confronted him, he turned the conversation around: "You must be having an affair if you are asking me such an absurd question."

I finally took my head out of the sand and followed my woman's intuition. I desperately needed answers so I started searching for any clues. I felt that his emails would tell me the story. Although his desktop computer was locked, I was finally able to figure out his password.

As I opened his emails, I felt as though my heart was beating out of my chest. What I found seemed like it was coming from a bad Lifetime television movie. My suspicions about Liam's fidelity, or lack thereof, were confirmed. And the really bitter irony was that I actually was in some ways the "other woman." He had been in an ongoing relationship for years with a woman he had been living with prior to being involved with me; it continued after we married.

I was stunned, horrified, and pissed. All I could think was, "How could Liam do this to me? I moved across the country from everything I have ever known." But I needed to know more. I tracked down her contact information, but I just held onto it at first. I was able to keep my cool for a day, not letting Liam know what I had found out about his betrayal.

The next day I asked to use his cellphone, walked into the other room, and dialed the number of his mistress. I placed his phone on speaker, and asked Liam if he knew a woman named Eileen (name changed). Of course, he said no. Then she answered her telephone: "Hello, darling, I miss you so much."

"Hello, Eileen, I'm Liam's wife; who are you? And what are you doing sending my husband all of those provocative emails and making Valentine's Day dinner and movie reservations?" That was the beginning of the end.

Even though I was still in love with Liam, I loved and respected myself more. After the trauma with my family, I had made a promise to myself to love myself first and never allow anyone to hurt, harm, or take advantage of me ever again. I knew our marriage was over and taking care of myself and keeping safe became my sole priority.

A few days later, I secretly scheduled local movers and two local sheriff officers to meet me at my home at a specific time and date. They knocked on the front door, and Liam answered. He was now looking at two officers and three large men from the moving company. As Liam stood at the entry wondering what was going on, I gently tapped him on his shoulder and looked directly into his eyes: "Oh, honey, I forgot to tell you, I am moving today."

He had no idea I was going to leave him because I had nothing packed and left no clues that I was finished with him forever. Plus, I did not know anyone in the entire state of Florida.

At that moment, the movers and officers stepped inside the house. I began to give instructions to the movers as the officers oversaw the entire process as a safety and wellness check. Hours later, as the sun began to set, we were finally finished. All of my personal belongings were in storage. As I sat in my car alone at the storage facility, I thought: "I have to stay focused on my emotional, spiritual, and physical well-being. Keep looking ahead, Carolyn, never give up, and don't look back."

Then I checked myself into a hotel.

NEVER ALLOW FEAR TO HOLD YOU BACK

Why have I shared this story with you in-depth? There are several reasons. First, I was an accomplished woman who thought I had taken my time and done my due diligence before getting married. I really, truly thought I knew Liam. But life can blindside you. Just as a simple toe stub turned out to be an injury that would lead to years of pain, my honest love for a man I trusted implicitly turned into something so wrong and abusive.

Could I have seen it coming? Could I have predicted the future? I can honestly answer no. But no one can predict the future. And I also know that hardening my heart and approaching all relationships with skepticism and distrust is not in my nature, nor do I ever want to live that closed-off kind of life.

Additionally, if I hadn't worked on tapping into my deep beauty and inner worth and, most importantly, focused on self-care, I could have wallowed in self-pity. In fact, given the accumulated trauma in just a few short years caused by my family, the loss of my beloved father, and the physical ailments that were now plaguing my body, I could have easily taken a nose dive and given up on life.

I chose not to. *I am the person who is responsible for my life, joy, happiness, and health.* For years, I had worked very hard on my total well-being by developing the necessary mindset with deep determination: by staying laser-focused on my mental, emotional, physical, financial, and spiritual health and growth.

By the time this experience with Liam took place, I had already done a lot of self-work in developing my inner strength and courage—never looking back or down, walking forward toward the light, believing in myself, and knowing that God was taking care of me completely.

I focused on my purpose with the mission of writing books and working to change laws that would help benefit family caregivers. I had a lot of beautiful work to do to make a difference in the world. I remained in Florida, eventually moving two hundred miles away to a location that provided me the lifestyle I wanted and reminded me of California. I discovered a small beach town that met my emotional, spiritual, and physical needs. Yes, I found the perfect place, just for me. I felt at home.

By the way, you may be wondering what happened to Liam. A few months after I left him, he was served with divorce papers—on his birthday. By summer, our divorce was final. Over time, I was able to forgive him completely. And today I genuinely wish him well.

Here's the thing about forgiveness: It has enormous power to help you take charge of your life. Without forgiveness, you will find yourself stuck in the past. Not being able to forgive will eat away at your deep beauty and inner worth. It will put a strong wall between your desire to practice self-care and your ability to really take action.

But the person I had to work hardest at forgiving was myself. I questioned my judgment. I wondered if I was totally naïve. Over and over I asked why I had made such a mistake. I was ruthless in looking at myself.

Now, one thing I want to stress is that self-reflection is a good thing. There are always multiple perspectives on a story. Did I make mistakes in my marriage? Absolutely. No relationship is without challenges. In the end, however, I knew my own truth. And that truth would not allow a liar and cheat in my life. I could forgive, but I could never forget my own values.

HOW TO GET RID OF PEOPLE WHO ARE HAZARDOUS TO YOUR HEALTH

We all have had a "Liam" in our life. Maybe it was a spouse or partner. Maybe it was a parent or child. Maybe it was a boss. Maybe it was a friend. Few of us escape being hurt by people we love or think we love.

We often believe that the first thing we need to do is get rid of those people who are hazardous to our health. That is the right thing to do—but it can also be very difficult, especially if the person is a child or family member. However, unless you start transforming yourself through self-care and tapping into your deep beauty and inner worth, you will probably repeat the same scenario in your next relationship. You will choose different people who are hazardous to your health.

So you need to be very conscious about whom you let into your life and how you deal with them if they are not good for you. I believe one of the most important ways to do that is by changing negative thoughts to positive ones. We will be talking about this idea throughout the book, but for now keep these five things in mind:

1. Let go of things you cannot change.
2. Love yourself.
3. Have compassion.

4. Practice acts of forgiveness.
5. Lead a purpose-filled life.

I also want to strongly remind you that *any form of abuse is never okay*. Anyone from any race, sexual orientation, age, gender, or religion can be a victim—or perpetrator—of abuse. Abuse can happen to people who are married, living together, just dating, friends, and family members. If you or someone you know is experiencing abuse, call the National Domestic Violence Hotline at 1-800-799-7233 | 1-800-787-3224 (TTY).

Getting out of abusive relationships often starts with having an aha moment—the kind of moment I had when I finally acknowledged that Liam was having an affair. But having the moment is not enough. You have to take action. And often you need the help of others to take that action.

In the next chapter, I will discuss aha moments in-depth. But I urge you right now: If you are being abused, do not wait for a revelation. Find the resources you need to remove yourself from the situation safely.

"RELATIONSHIP SELF-CARE" QUESTIONS

Think about your views regarding relationships and how they have affected your health and life. In your personal binder or on your computer, start writing your thoughts and answer the following questions. Remember, take all the time you need. This is your journey and your life.

1. How would you describe your relationships with the most important people in your life? Who are they? What are your expectations? And are they meeting them?
2. Are you happy with your partner? Why? Or why not?
3. What do you think is missing in your relationship? What steps do you have in mind to improve your relationship? List them.
4. Do you see signs of emotional, financial, or physical abuse? If so, what are they?
5. What are your deal breakers? And why?
6. Do you feel safe? If not, why? List the reasons. Have you asked for help yet?
7. Have you thought about conversations you would like to have with your partner or other loved ones? If so, what do you plan to discuss? What outcome are you expecting?
8. Do you suspect infidelity? If so, why? How do you plan to move forward?

9. Have you and your spouse looked for professionals with expertise in family relationships? If so, when was your first appointment? What were the results and action plan?

10. Are you taking the time you need to work on yourself, emotionally, physically, financially, and spiritually? If so, how?

11. Do you remember the last time you and your partner went on a date? Or a getaway? Or a vacation? What's stopping you from going on one? And where would you go?

12. If you have to move forward from an abusive situation, are you ready to transform your life through self-care, by tapping into your deep beauty for inner strength?

When Aha Moments
Become Defining Moments

$\mathcal{R}$emember the last time you experienced a thought-provoking aha moment? You know, that particular moment that suddenly gives you a clear vision or specific understanding that can change in an instant everything you've been thinking about. I have shared a few of mine so far relating to my health, job, family, and husband.

We all have experienced them. When you recognize these mind-blowing flashes of clarity, suddenly things in your life will start making better sense and provide you with the power to shift your thinking to greater possibilities.

Everyone's aha experience may be considerably different. You may have experienced your aha moments while taking a shower, driving, exercising, sleeping, fishing, or wherever you are feeling relaxed. For me, I discovered that my aha moments typically occur in the wee hours of the morning, around 3:30 a.m. That is when my mind has gone deep beneath the surface of everything I have thought about during the day.

Often, my aha moment awakens me with the most brilliant thoughts and ideas. Because of this, it has become imperative for me to have a pen and paper ready—next to me on my nightstand—since I never know when my epiphany might visit. I know these moments are extraordinary and essential for nurturing the aha moment that taps into the deep beauty of my soul.

I have been asked many times, "Carolyn, how did you reach the aha moments that changed your life?" My reply is quite simple.

I start by making clarity of my mind, body, and spirit a top priority. I am able to achieve clarity of the mind by permitting myself *not to think* about anything that is unsettling to my soul. I do not force my mind to push through difficult situations or deal with troublesome issues that are out of my control. I let go.

Instead of worrying, I incorporate activities of relaxation for my mind, body, and spirit. I embrace the precious moments that nature provides by taking long walks on the beach and by gardening. I practice meditation or working out. I enjoy therapeutic bubble baths. I spend quality time alone.

Know that your thoughts are powerful. Frequently, because of our daily hectic schedules, it is easy to forget about the importance of creating the "me time" that is essential for mental clarity. Plan your me time. Try aiming for at least an hour per day. You can take your time at once or divide that hour into small intervals that work best for you. I enjoy the mornings, which seem always to provide me peace and tranquility.

Make peace of mind your top priority, and find a quiet place just for you. It could be in your home, library, or anywhere that provides solitude and relaxation. Once you find that place, start focusing on your inner thoughts by going deep beneath the surface of what's happening around you. Give yourself permission to think about nothing except things that relax your mind, body, and soul. You can learn and master this technique through mindful meditation.

Once I have had my me time for the day, I can focus, organize, and be more productive. Practicing this approach to clarity enables me to have full access to my mind, body, and spirit. It allows me to have many special and insightful moments.

HOW AHA MOMENTS WORK

I have become fascinated by what conditions provoke moments of clarity and how your brain works to create these moments. One of the gurus on this topic is David Rock, who coined the term "neuroleadership" and is the author of many books, including *Your Brain at Work: Strategies for Overcoming Distraction, Regaining Focus, and Working Smarter All Day Long.*

Recently he and another researcher, Josh Davis, articulated four steps to having more aha moments. Their conclusions, which closely align with my own, are:

1. Notice quiet signals: Allow silence and solitude in your life daily.
2. Look within: Focus on your inner thoughts and overlook the noise around you.
3. Take a positive approach: Feeling even slightly happy is conducive to problem solving.
4. Use less effort: Stepping away from deliberation is critical for quality decision-making.[1]

Science also backs up the idea that our minds operate differently during aha moments. Researcher Mark Jung-Beeman notes that brain activity changes when creative insight takes hold. Specifically, moments of clarity result in expanded activity in a small part of the right lobe of the brain called the temporal lobe. That is the part that is vital for drawing distantly related information together, which is crucial for insight.[2]

While I am not a researcher, I have conducted my own interviews with thousands of people who have read my books over the last decade. I asked them what triggered their own aha moments.

For some, aha moments were experience-driven. For example, one person woke up anxious every day, with her mind racing through the things she needed to do. Then she didn't do them. One morning she got up, wrote her list of things down, and started trying to get through them. The next morning, she woke up peaceful even though she hadn't finished most of the items on her list. She realized that procrastinating—not the actual list of things—was causing her anxiety. That was her aha moment. Now when she feels anxious, she writes down the things she needs to do, tackles a few, crosses them off, and makes a list of other things she did get done. It has helped.

Interestingly, this aha moment about lists is supported by research. For example, Roy Baumeister and E. J. Masicampo, professors from Wake Forest University, found that just making a plan—writing down the tasks—significantly reduces anxiety.[3]

Here's a truth about our world. A significant amount of our knowledge comes from aha moments that became insights that became scientifically validated facts.

Another woman recently relayed a profound aha moment that she had as a result of having broken her shoulder. Naomi (name changed) is known professionally for her aha moments in the shower. This is the time when her creativity and insights run deep. Her clients often ask her what ideas she got that day in the shower.

Naomi is highly intellectual with a thirst for knowledge and a mind that is always racing. In terms of self-care, she has read countless books on diet and exercise. But her journey has been very up and down; she carries more than one hundred pounds of extra weight.

Her experience-based aha moment came from not being able to use her primary arm. She has come to realize that distraction is her enemy and deliberate actions are her friend. She has to type with her left hand, so her writing process has become more focused—although tedious. If she is talking and walking, she risks bumping her hurt arm. She needs to get up and down from a chair using her stomach muscles instead of her arms. Everything needs to be deliberate, and she now realizes that what she puts in her body should also be based on mindfulness. She continues to put her aha moment into action.

So as you see, actions create aha moments. My own back pain, going to a psychologist, and discovery of my husband's infidelity all provided me with aha moments that profoundly changed my life.

THE WHY QUESTION

For many people, however, aha moments come from a conscious search for clarity. What I have discovered from my own research is that the number-one reason that people give for having an aha moment is the desire to find out the answer to a "why" question: Why did this happen? In fact, people spend years trying to make sense of the why question.

The fact of the matter is that you may never get an answer until you can relax your mind, body, and spirit. For many years, I thought about my past, forever questioning the why as well. I was trying to use my intellect to figure it all out. I wanted to resolve certain questions I had regarding struggles in my life. Nonetheless, I was miserable because I could not find the answers in a textbook or by talking to friends, family, or even my psychologist. I felt as if I was locked in an imaginary prison in my mind by not having the answers.

One morning I was awakened by the most amazing inner soft voice. At that moment, I discovered my miracle—the complete understanding of the why question I had carried around with me for years. I recognized my mental prison doors were finally open. And boy, did I walk through the why doors toward the bright and shining light of just knowing.

At that moment, I understood the reason behind the trials and tribulations I had endured in my past. I began to understand the divine reason for my life's journey: Its purpose was to make a difference in the world. Just knowing this valuable information closed those mental prison doors behind me forever. And I never asked my why question ever again.

It was one of the most remarkable aha moment I had ever experienced. It was a defining moment. Having this knowledge helped me transmute negative thoughts to power and strength with the determination of creating life-changing solutions. It has fueled my creative thoughts and taken me to the higher calling of my divine purpose and mission.

TURNING AHA MOMENTS INTO DEFINING MOMENTS

Your own aha moment doesn't need to be about changing the world, though. It could be about how to tackle one small problem that has been hounding you, or it could be just recognizing what is holding you back from success, big or small. The thing is to recognize the moment as a turning point, perhaps the end of one chapter and the beginning of a new one.

I remember reading an article in *Psychology Today* in which psychology experts shared their personal aha moments. This one by Susan Newman stood out for me: "For no apparent reason, a close friend called to end our decades-old friendship. I was distraught and asked why. She refused any discussion and stopped taking my calls. After months of feeling terrible and wondering what I had done, it hit me: This wasn't about me; it was her issue. That realization taught me to not assume blame too quickly. In many emotional struggles, the problem revolves around someone else's needs more than mine (or yours)."[4] The key to an effective aha moment is learning from it—recognizing it as a moment of insight and power, owning it, and acting on it.

As I mentioned, my own desire to understand aha moments has spurred my informal survey of the thousands of people I talk with every year. I have been particularly interested in defining moments—those moments that profoundly affect the course of your journey.

During my international talk radio show I was interviewing Lashai, a fifteen-year-old from London, England. I was amazed at how brilliant, talented, and mature she was. At that time, she had written several books and was on many television shows.

I asked Lashai, "How did you develop so much passion, for being so young?" She said, "My passion is my mission that my soul defines." Oh my goodness, just think about how powerful and profound that statement is. That is one interview that will stay with me forever.

Here are the top fifty statements that people have shared with me about aha moments that helped them define their lives. These life-defining moments are not in ranking order, but all have deep meaning to me:

1. "You understand that the good stuff that matters are the simple things that took a lifetime to achieve, like raising a child."
2. "When I face my fears, it's like walking up to a roaring lion and discovering the lion has no teeth."
3. "It's okay to do absolutely nothing and not feel guilty."
4. "To embrace my uniqueness and look at it as a blessing."
5. "It's not the stuff in life that matters; what matters are those precious moments with our loved ones."
6. "When I am confronted with challenges or problems at work, I look at them as temporary situations that will be solved."
7. "I have to create better relationships with my family, friends, and coworkers by empowering open exchanges and demonstrating more appreciation."

8. "I understand overbooking myself takes a huge toll on my mind, body, and spirit, so I need to safeguard my calendar."
9. "I can let go of the things that are out of my control."
10. "Forgiving is not just for the benefit of the other person; forgiving frees my soul."
11. "I can recognize my aha moments when they come."
12. "I take full responsibility for my happiness and know that I am the only one responsible for it."
13. "I am my only competition. I will stop comparing myself with others."
14. "Feeding my soul with inspirational knowledge is the beacon in my life."
15. "I must stop depending on others for my safekeeping."
16. "I am no longer going to feel guilty for taking care of me."
17. "I need to do my part by practicing self-care so I can be a greater example to my kids."
18. "I will learn to say no and not feel guilty."
19. "I cannot change my spouse, but I can change me."
20. "Giving to others gives me an amazing feeling that money can't buy."
21. "I will quit giving myself excuses for not eating healthy, not exercising, or not taking care of me."
22. "I will listen more to what my body is telling me and act on it."
23. "It's my responsibility to love myself regardless of my past."
24. "Chasing money isn't everything. Being an active part of my kids' lives means the world to me."
25. "My life is really a beautiful blessing, and now I embrace it."
26. "In order to get results, I must apply effort."
27. "I will treat my loved one special every day, because we never know when that last day is coming."
28. "My aha moment is my moment and is not meant for others to understand."
29. "I need to work on loving myself more so I can give more love to others."
30. "I'm not going to focus on the stresses of the world but create my own happiness and share it."
31. "I am in charge of inspiring and empowering my team at work, and I accept the challenge."
32. "I need to give myself permission to celebrate my success and embrace the joy."
33. "A vacation is not a vacation when I am constantly checking email and social media daily."
34. "I look in the mirror and see the beautiful person I *am*."

35. "I will look at solutions versus focusing on problems."
36. "Not all questions will have an answer, but in time things will start making better sense."
37. "I want to become healthy and stop focusing on being a size two."
38. "It's not my responsibility to control the lives of other adults."
39. "My talents are a gift from heaven."
40. "Some relationships are not meant to last forever."
41. "I need to practice showing more empathy to build stronger relationships."
42. "Discovering my life's purpose gives my existence more meaning."
43. "I will seek out positive people, places, and things to incorporate in my life."
44. "I finally recognize why self-care is so important, and I'm going for it."
45. "I've learned to embrace happiness wherever I go."
46. "The opinions other people hold of me do not define me."
47. "Nothing lasts forever. I must enjoy the moment."
48. "I will embrace my special gifts and realize they are a blessing."
49. "I *am* a creator of wonderful things. I've just got to do it."
50. "I will never miss an opportunity for greatness when my aha moments arrive."

One of the themes you can see from these statements is that they often lead to a defining moment about the importance of self-care. But here is the rub: *Defining moments that are not translated into action really don't move you ahead to having a better life.* They do not transform you in real ways that let you thrive and be happy.

As the French author George Bernanos said, "A thought which does not result in an action is nothing much, and an action which does not proceed from a thought is nothing at all."[5]

So what stops people from turning defining moments into self-care actions? In the next chapter, I will explore the reasons why we resist self-care.

"AHA MOMENTS SELF-CARE" QUESTIONS

Think about the last time you experienced an aha moment. How did it affect your thinking? What were the actions that followed? In your personal binder, start writing your thoughts by answering the following questions. Remember to take all the time you need. This is your journey and your life.

1. When did you recognize you were having an aha moment?
2. How are you balancing work, family, and self-care?
3. What activities spark your defining moments?
4. How do you plan to create your "me" time?
5. Have you experienced a missed opportunity because you did not take action when you had an aha moment? What was it?
6. Do you believe that aha moments spark your creative energy? If so, describe your life-defining moments.
7. Have you discovered your divine purpose and life mission due to an aha moment? If so, how did you discover it, and what is your divine purpose?
8. Have you ever had an aha moment about facing something that you fear? If so, what did you fear? And what was your defining moment?
9. What is your passion? What is your soul calling you to do?
10. What was the aha moment that allowed you to tap into your deep beauty and inner worth? And what was the outcome of your defining moment?
11. What actions have you taken in response to an aha moment? How did those actions turn out?

· *4* ·

Why We Resist Self-Care

$\mathcal{I}$ will be the first to admit that I used to be guilty of resisting self-care, too. Why? I had every reason you can imagine, and probably many of the same reasons most people have. I was far too busy. I did not have the time. I'd get around to it later. It was too expensive.

Here's the truth: All my reasons seemed completely valid to me. My living expenses were enormous. I was a caregiver for my dad. I had a demanding career in the pharmaceutical industry. I had very little spare time.

And here's the other truth: All my reasons were completely false. The real reasons why I resisted self-care ran much deeper. That's what I want to talk with you about in this chapter. When you realize that your reasons for not taking care of yourself are deeper than the everyday excuses, your aha moment will come. Then you will eliminate the everyday excuses because you will absolutely want to wrap yourself in self-love.

MY RECKONING AND AHA MOMENT

Let's talk about what happened to me for a few moments. For many years, I overlooked little telltale health signals that were telling me to slow down or stop. I just kept going day after day. I worked through pain. I worked through injuries. I ignored doctors' advice.

On some level, I thought I was a superwoman. Why not? I saw myself as young, healthy, and full of energy. I was successful and disciplined in my work. Others perceived me as highly competent and efficient. I was juggling many things and was sure I was doing it well. I believed it, and so did the people around me.

Then I ended up as a patient in an orthopedic surgeon's practice due to excruciating back pain. On one of my visits, he gave me a referral to see a clinical psychologist. I immediately resisted his recommendation. In fact, I was quite put out: "What does my chronic back pain have to do with seeing a psychologist? I'm coming to you to make me better. That's your job."

The doctor disagreed strongly: "Ms. Brent, this is part of your self-care. Your body has been traumatized, and you might never be the same again. In fact, your condition may get worse as you age. I always recommend my patients speak with a clinical psychologist when they are facing life-changing health conditions."

Even though my doctor told me that I could end up in a wheelchair due to the damage I had done to my back and that my life would be changed forever, I resisted the idea of seeing a psychologist for weeks. Then I decided to comply with his recommendation. I can't exactly tell you why. Maybe it was to prove him wrong. Maybe it was because I was feeling desperate and would try anything. Maybe it was divine intervention. I don't really know why, but I can tell you that I immediately felt comfortable during my first appointment with the clinical psychologist. I was in the right place.

During our discussions, I became more aware of why I had resisted seeing him. He helped me understand my resistance may have come from the stigma surrounding mental health. He explained how I needed to start looking at myself as a whole person, not just a caregiver, daughter, and working professional. He showed me that life was more than just the hamster endlessly running at a fast pace on a treadmill. He also provided me with reading material for total self-care and recommended that I start journaling. Since that day, I have journaled daily.

I will never forget his words, which now seem so obvious but at the time were profound: "You are a person with real feelings that needed to be addressed."

Eventually, I opened up, realizing just how frightened I was about my health and future. I began to understand how I had swallowed my emotions from the battles I faced with my family, career, and chronic back pain. Most importantly, I wanted to learn how to take my power back, because along the way I had forgotten how important self-care was for me.

Months later, I was blown away when I realized that my visit with a psychologist was my first intentional act of not resisting self-care. Had I not followed through with the orthopedic surgeon's recommendation, I may not have experienced the aha moment that prompted me to take a closer look at me—the whole person, mind, body, and spirit.

In essence, going to see a psychologist was the affirmation I needed for the clarity of the gamut of emotions that I held deep within my soul. I was ready to take action toward total self-care. This initial act led me to my continuous transformation and healing.

Now I look at self-care as the first-line treatment for my mind, body, and spirit. I recognize self-care is a form of self-love. It helps me resist sickness, poverty, depression, guilt, and self-sabotage. Since my first visit, I've learned how to live and thrive in the world we live in, in spite of what's going on around me. I no longer resist. I embrace.

I believe we can look at the word "resist" as a powerful tool that can lead to desiring more knowledge and information. Resisting self-care is an indicator of a lack of clarity and understanding about the importance of it. Learning the reason why you resist self-care is critical for you to experience a more vibrant and healthier existence in every area of your life. The knowledge will provide you with more focus and clarity and motivate you toward greater life improvements.

Frequently, we resist the unknown, not realizing that self-care is accessible to anyone who wants it. Are you ready to do the necessary work toward self-care? And are you aware that self-care does not have an end date? Yes, I did say you have to do the work and there isn't an end date. But know that eventually your mind, body, and spirit will start to crave the benefits of self-care. Self-care will not feel like work when the act of self-care becomes your lifestyle.

There is another very important message to my story that I want you to really take to heart: I waited until I did irreparable damage to my body to start practicing self-care. Since then, I have managed the pain and actually reversed some of the problems, but my body *did not* have to get the point it did before I got help.

Don't make the mistake I made. Start practicing self-care now. Don't wait.

THE FEAR FACTORS OF SELF-CARE

So why do people wait? I have told you my story, but I believe that it may all come down to fear. That's the theme I hear in the thousands of people I talk to each year. Fear related to personal issues such as health, money matters, physical abilities or disabilities, self-confidence, lack of discipline, and the judgment of others. Fear of losing control over your time. Fear of the effort involved in self-care.

Maybe self-care means stepping out of your comfort zone. Are you protecting your boundaries? Could it be that you may not want to relinquish your bad habits or your privacy? Do you have a challenge with adjusting to new routines? Or could it be that you are hiding a chronic illness or condition?

Have you accepted as a core belief the idea that self-care is too hard? Or that self-care is just for athletes? Or that self-care is only for rich and famous people who can afford it? Or that self-care is just for the educated? Or that putting yourself first makes you a selfish person?

I have found that caregivers, in particular, think that putting yourself first makes you a selfish person. Often, for example, young mothers who were previously into self-care and were passionate about their health during pregnancy will not take care of themselves once their children are born. They will feel selfish about leaving their children with a babysitter so they can go to the gym. They will grab quick meals because they are so absorbed with taking care of their child. They try to do it all and end up exhausted physically, emotionally, and spiritually. Self-care has gone to the bottom of their priority list at the time when they probably need it the most.

Would any of these moms tolerate someone calling them selfish? I don't think so. But that is exactly what they are calling themselves—or would call themselves, if they practiced self-care. Remember that words have power. The words you use define your beliefs and who you think you are.

Have you found yourself making any of these statements with regard to self-care?

- I fear failure.
- It makes me feel too selfish.
- I feel guilty.
- I am miserable.
- I am poor.
- It's too hard.
- I can't break my bad habits.
- I don't want to face the real truth about my health.
- Why me?
- What I don't know about my health can't hurt me.
- It's hard for me to do my part.
- I am fearful of the unknown.
- I am afraid of what people will think about me.
- I am going to die of something anyway.
- I am too old.
- I can't change.
- My family is just unhealthy. It's in the cards.
- I don't deserve to take care of myself.
- I don't have the time.

These are all damaging and self-fulfilling excuses. The list goes on and on. But you have it in your power to change your language and attitude. You can step up to the plate now by doing all you can to help yourself. Or do you want to depend on your family and friends? Or wait for the healthcare system to take care of you? Is that what you really want?

Here's the thing about excuses (and believe me, over the last ten years I have heard every one of them from people of all ages, genders, nationalities, and cultural and/or socioeconomic backgrounds): Excuses sound like truth to us. They seem as real as the sun, ocean, and sky. But the real truth is more like oxygen. We need it to survive, but we don't see it. We have to learn about it and change our beliefs to accept what we don't see.

To practice self-care, you have to find your truth. Why are you being so thoughtless to the only body you have? Why are you treating yourself so cruelly? Why don't you treat yourself with love?

We can all come up with many reasons for resisting self-care. But what happens when you do not take care of yourself? The effects can be quite devastating. Just remember, I am a living witness to what can happen when you resist self-care. And I am also a living witness to what can happen when you embrace self-care.

I'd like to address four excuses specifically that I find very prominent among people who do not practice self-care. Even if they are not saying these statements aloud, they are stuck in people's brains.

1. I am too old.
2. I can't change.
3. My family is just unhealthy. It's in the cards.
4. I don't deserve to take care of myself.

"I AM TOO OLD" EXCUSE

I can't tell you how many times I have heard people say they are too old to take care of themselves. They may have been athletic as teenagers but gave up on good eating and exercise as they got older. They placed their family first. They got wrapped up in their career. They don't really care how they look anymore because they are no longer trying to find a significant other. Quite simply, often men and women "let themselves go" in middle age, and then feel they are too old to make changes in their lifestyles.

Here's the kicker: Growing older is a part of life. You've got to start looking beyond your life now and instead see where you will be in the future. We all hope to live long and healthy lives, which requires taking action. Nobody wants to end up in a nursing home, but here's the bitter truth. It is a myth that nursing homes and long-term care facilities are just for old people. I challenge you to go and visit a local nursing home near you. You will see that long-term care facilities are for all ages.

So do you really want to end up in a nursing facility in your fifties or sixties? Do you want to be able to play with your kids in your forties? Do you want to travel the world in comfort and be able to play with your grandkids when you retire?

And what will happen to you if you don't have a strong family or friend network? Who will take care of you if you age poorly?

I will forever believe that how you take care of yourself or do not take care of yourself will eventually catch up with you later in life. However, you should never use your age as an excuse. Remember, it's not where you start, it's all about taking action now and how you finish.

The following article title immediately caught my attention when it was published: "No Spouse, No Kids, No Caregiver: How to Prepare to Age Alone." It was written by Anna Medaris Miller, a health and wellness editor at *U.S. News*. Her article talks about the growing population of "elder or-phans" who lack a built-in support system and what to do if you become one.

The article cites a 2012 study in *The Gerontologist*, that estimates that about one-third of forty-five- to sixty-three-year-olds are single, most of whom either never married or are divorced. That's a whopping 50 percent increase since 1980. What's more is that about 15 percent of forty- to forty-four-year-old women had no children in 2012, up from about 10 percent in 1980 in the United States. The question the elder orphans are asking is, "How in the world will we take care of ourselves?"[1]

But age does not need to be a factor. You may have already heard about the story of Ernestine Shepherd. Born on June 16, 1936, she is famous for being one of the oldest competitive female body builders in the world. She started her career in her late fifties. As of 2018, she is eighty-two years old and still an active, albeit no longer competitive, bodybuilder.[2]

I have a phenomenal wellness and fitness guru who acted as my personal cheerleader when I competed on the National Physical Committee (NPC) stage. Meet my dear friend, seventy-one-year-old Dr. Josefina Monasterio, an NPC Bodybuilder Women's Champion. She started training as a pro-fessional body builder at age fifty-nine. She firmly believes that you can be empowered at any age. She said, "Muster the inspiration, determination, discipline, and energy to make those changes that will propel you to your next level. Reinvent yourself as you feel in your gut that your development and per-fection is working. Become the co-creator with the eternity of your destiny."[3]

THE "I CAN'T CHANGE" EXCUSE

It is challenging to understand why change can be so difficult, especially when it is to our benefit. Dr. Ralph Ryback, a contributor to *Psychology Today News*, describes it well:

> As creatures of habit, we often have difficulty incorporating new changes into our routines, no matter how beneficial they are for us, because we tend to do the things that make us feel good, secure and comfortable. Even when we are motivated and make reasonable efforts to change, why is it that we are still so resistant to changing our behavior, even when these changes are healthy or beneficial to us?[4]

He explains that our inertia works against us in achieving our goals. Surprisingly, inertia is an overlooked concept when it comes to understanding our inherent complex resistance to losing weight or beginning a new exercise routine. Inertia helps to describe why our bodies tend to act against us when we try to begin a new diet or an exercise routine.[5]

Often, inertia and reluctance to change cross generations. But it doesn't have to keep on going. I'd like to share some stories of clients who broke the cycle of generational poor health through self-care.

Sarah's self-care challenges began in her early teens. She was born into a hardworking American family that believed you work hard, play hard, but never waste food. Because of her family's beliefs, everyone in her family was morbidly overweight. Her family had also accepted that being overweight was not a big deal and nutrition was not a top priority or concern. They centered their lives on the belief that family love is to be celebrated around the idea of "*eat, drink, and be happy.*"

By the time Sarah was a senior in high school, she was forty-five pounds overweight and suffering from poor self-esteem and self-image issues. Her high school dream to become a cheerleader was lost when she could not make the team. But that did not stop Sarah from going after another dream to pursue a degree in journalism.

Four years later, Sarah graduated from college and began her career in journalism as an intern with a major newspaper, where a well-respected wellness journalist mentored her. Her assignments covered health and wellness businesses in New York City.

That was when Sarah recognized that she needed to learn more about her own health, wellness, and nutrition. She was ready to transform her life, tapping into her deep beauty and inner worth. She wanted to break the cycle of obesity and the accepted medical issues that ran rampant in her family as "normal." More importantly, Sarah wanted to share her newfound health and self-care benefits with her family, so they could change.

One year later, Sarah lost forty-five pounds and has successfully kept it off. She is now a "cheerleader" for good health, wellness, and nutrition to her family—breaking the cycle of poor eating habits. She has become an agent for change.

THE DNA EXCUSE

One of the most common reasons I hear for people not practicing self-care is their family health history. "We've always had bad backs." "People in my family tend to be fat." "Nobody has ever lived past 60." "Cancer runs in my family." "My parents both had heart problems, so I expect I will too."

I'm not saying that self-care is going to change your DNA, but what I am saying is that you have to fight for your health. And you have to see yourself growing older and enjoying your quality of life with good health. That is why you must take action and never allow anything or anyone ever to stop you. You've got to develop and own a made-up mind that self-care is for you.

I know this from firsthand experience. I was born into a family with life-threatening health issues such as hereditary heart disease, hypertension, high cholesterol, type 2 diabetes, and dementia. My mother and three of my siblings all died from heart attacks. First, my mother passed at age sixty-three, followed by two brothers at ages fifty-four and fifty-three and then my younger sister at age forty-nine. Yes, this is a very sad but sobering family statistic.

Just knowing my bloodline and the DNA that I was born with has helped me to be proactive in doing my part regarding self-care. It is my responsibility to pursue the knowledge I need to help transform my health. I have learned to fight the good fight of faith by doing all I can do toward self-care. The good news is that I know my family history, which gives me a fighting chance to actively live a healthier life. You do not have to resign yourself to a family history; you can recognize it, learn about it, and balance it out with healthy approaches to those threats.

Here's some more good news: You too can start today and place self-care as your number-one priority by taking action now. In time, your self-care results will deliver you the benefits of a more energetic and healthier life, no matter what your DNA. With awareness and information, you can pass on the knowledge of self-care as an inheritance to your children and your children's children.

THE "I DON'T DESERVE IT" EXCUSE

You may wonder if people actually say this statement. Unfortunately, they do. Sometimes, they say they don't have time or ability, but if you probe deeper, they will say that they really don't believe they deserve to take care of themselves. They are not worthy.

This excuse breaks my heart. And I hear it way too often, especially among women. What has happened in your life that you actually believe you are not worthy and don't deserve to take care of yourself?

I don't believe there is a quick fix to overcome this excuse. I think you have to do in-depth work to find your deep beauty and inner worth, and you may need professional help on this issue.

But here's an interesting phenomenon: If you start practicing self-care—even if you feel you don't deserve it—your self-esteem and sense of worth may increase. Essentially, taking a "fake it until you make it" approach may actually be a terrific strategy to get you thinking more positively about yourself.

The enhancement of self-esteem and self-efficacy can be an important contributing factor to both the prevention of psychological and physical illness and the maintenance of health. Specifically, researchers have found exercise contributes to the prevention of illness or the reduction of its effects through the process of improving self-esteem.[6]

I have a client named Aharon, who is a tremendously successful businessman. He started his own company at nineteen and has never worked for anyone. Aharon is now sixty-four years old.

His family immigrated to the United States in the early 1940s. They were very poor and held on to every penny they ever got their hands on. But the tighter they held onto their money, the more it seemed to squeeze out of their hands like sand falling on the ground, leaving them consistently at a stage of lacking. They lived a life of emotional, physical, and spiritual poverty because they felt that their lifestyle was as good as it would ever get.

Aharon told me that he knew he had a different mindset from his parents. At age nine he thought, "I don't want to be like my parents. My parents do not think they deserve a better life. They have settled for a life of poverty and hardship."

Aharon was destined to break the family cycle of poverty because he had a made-up mind at a very early age that poverty was not for him. He had the deep discipline to create a better life for himself and the generations to follow. In 2008 Aharon moved to Haiti for a year, contributing his talents and finances to rebuilding Haiti and helping save the lives of children and their parents. He has helped communities worldwide and broken the cycle of "the poverty of the mind" in his own family.

A leader of the "You Can" movement, he believed he deserved a better life and now shows others how to vanquish the "I don't deserve it" excuse.

THE POWER OF YOUR WORDS

We have talked about the negative power of words. Conversely, the positive power of words is not to be underestimated. According to Dr. Ronald Alexander, author of *Wise Mind, Open Mind*, "Affirmations (statements said with confidence about a perceived truth) have helped thousands of people make significant changes in their lives. But they don't always work for everyone. How can one person have great success using this tool, while another sees no results at all? An affirmation can work because it has the ability to program your mind into believing the stated concept."

Dr. Alexander's research shows the five steps to make affirmations more effective and powerful:

1. Make a list of what you've always thought of as your negative qualities.
2. Write out an affirmation on the positive aspect of your self-judgment.
3. Speak the affirmation out loud for about five minutes, three times a day—morning, midday, and evening.
4. Anchor the affirmation in your body as you are repeating it by placing your hand on the area that felt uncomfortable when you wrote out the negative belief in step 1.
5. Get a friend or coach to repeat your affirmation to you.[7]

Never underestimate the power of your words to overcome your resistance to self-care. Be grateful for being uniquely created. You are an original and not a carbon copy. Speak positive powerful words of affirmation daily as your energy. Here are some examples:

- I am blessed.
- I am thankful.
- I am grateful for wisdom.
- I am a blessing to others.
- I am anointed.
- I am healthy.
- I am healed.
- I am a whole person.
- I am worth it.
- I am beautiful.

- I am loved.
- I am happy.
- I am positive.
- I am rich.
- I am worthy.
- I am the purity of love's desire.
- I am a magnificent beam of light.
- I am resilient.
- I am so glad to be me.
- I am unique and special.

One of my favorite quotes about self-care and proof of the power of words is by Wayne Dyer. It resonates in my soul every day: "You'll seldom experience regret for anything that you've done. It is what you haven't done that will torment you. The message, therefore, is clear. Do it! Develop an appreciation for the present moment. Seize every second of your life and savor it."[8]

In the next chapter, we will discuss how to commit to reclaiming your health.

"SELF-CARE RESISTANCE" QUESTIONS

Now it's your time to pull out your binder or computer and write about your wellness journey, from resisting self-care to embracing self-care. Answer the following questions to help you on your self care journey.

1. Have you checked with a trusted healthcare professional to assist you with your healthcare? If so, what recommendations were made? And how do you plan to get started?
2. Have you resisted the advice of your trusted healthcare professional? If so, why?
3. Are you resisting self-care? If so, why?
4. Have you ever given yourself excuses to resist self-care? If so, what were the excuses? And how do you plan to turn your excuses around to an action?
5. In what ways do you sabotage your self-care? Why do you think you do this?
6. What telltale signs or symptoms is your body displaying? Are you ignoring your symptoms? If so, why?
7. What is your greatest concern about your health? And how do you plan to address your concerns?

8. Are you experiencing fear, anxiety, or stress in taking care yourself? If so, what are your fears? And why do you think you are feeling this way? Have you spoken to a mental healthcare professional to get support?

9. Do you have a support team to assist you? If so, who are the members? If you do not have a support team, why not? And what are your plans to create one?

10. What are the five most powerful words of affirmation you can think of? Are you committed to speaking those affirmations daily? And what are the benefits for you?

11. Have you told yourself that you can commit to self-care? List five actions you can honestly commit to for this week.

• 5 •

Reclaiming Your Health

$\mathcal{R}$eclaiming your health is more than just wanting it. Or desiring it. Or dreaming about it. Or wishing for it. Reclaiming your health is about having an "I can-do" and "I must do" winning attitude.

You've got to take action. You've got to take back your authority. You've got to believe that your health belongs to you. You've got to see yourself healthier. You've got to feel and taste it. You've got to live it. You've got to trust yourself. You've got to make the commitment.

And you've got to do the work. When you do the work, your results will be waiting for you.

I believe that to be successful everyone needs to start with three things:

1. *Know your why.* Why do you really want to get healthy? Did you lose a friend to a preventable disease? Is your family genetics working against you? Do you want to achieve a goal that is hampered by poor health? Everyone has his or her why, and it is important to clearly understand what yours is. Knowing the primary reason for reclaiming your health is essential for you to plan and execute. If you don't know your why, you will be at a high risk of sabotaging your hard work. So take the time to educate, learn, and clarify your why. You may want to consult with a trusted healthcare professional to help you.

2. *Acknowledge your truth.* It is essential for you to acknowledge and be truthful about where your health is now. Then truthfully ask where would you like to see yourself in six months or one year from now. Tie your truth of where you are now and where you want to be into practical, life-enhancing goals. For example, I want to increase my upper body strength so I can do more work around my house and

41

garden. Or I want to increase my walking stamina so that I can tour Europe easier. Or I want to lose twenty pounds so I feel and look better for my son's graduation. Or I want to take a job with more traveling, and I want to develop the habits that will allow me to stay healthy when on the road.

3. *Develop and maintain a made-up mind.* You've got to take ownership of your life. Stop blaming everyone else and crummy past experiences. Stop looking for excuses. You've got to be tired of being depressed, stressed out, overweight, financially strained, overwhelmed, unhappy; feeling crummy; and having a life that is spiraling out of control. You need to be sick and tired of being sick and tired. Once that happens, you are ready to develop a made-up-mind attitude by transforming your thoughts into an "I can do," winning mindset. I believe it is harder to maintain a made-up mind than to develop one. Many of us wake up in the morning with a clear view of a new day. Or we have moments of clarity around occasions like birthdays or a new year. We are ready to start fresh and take ownership. But then our made-up mind turns to mush.

So what strategies can you put in place to keep a good attitude? First, don't go it alone. Surround yourself with supporters. Second, acknowledge that you will slip but absolutely commit to beginning again. Don't give yourself a week. Start immediately when you recognize that you have lost your attitude. Third, go back to your why. Remember why you are on a path of self-care.

HEAT UP YOUR ATTITUDE

Remember how we have discussed the power of words and affirmations? I want your house and office to become Affirmation Heaven. Put affirmations at eye level, where you can see them. Say them aloud. Every night pick one and journal about it. Immerse yourself in affirmations just like you are learning a new language—because you are: the language of you.

The following are the affirmations I suggest as you start your wellness journey.

- Today I take full responsibility and ownership of my life.
- Today I believe in my mission, and I am taking charge of my health.
- Today I will get my ego entirely out of my way.
- Today I will stop blaming others for my past mistakes and experiences.
- Today I forgive myself for not doing [. . .].

- Today I will not blame my parents, siblings, or other family members for what they did or did not do.
- Today I will not blame my former spouse(s) and/or friends who betrayed me.
- Today I will not blame my former employers who let me go.
- Today I will not blame anything or anyone who has ever hurt or harmed me.
- Today I am willing to learn.
- Today I am open-minded to new and healthier ways of living.
- Today I am committed to reclaiming my health and life.
- Today I believe I will succeed, and nothing will stop me.
- Today I plan to win, win, and win in reclaiming my health and freedom.

In addition to affirmations, surrounding yourself with inspiring quotes is another good way to heat up your attitude and keep the fire burning. Put these quotes around your house or workplace to help beautify the décor of your mind and heart.

I will be forever grateful for my dad, Pastor William L. Brent, the most wonderful and amazing parent I could have ever hoped or asked for. One of the most encouraging, uplifting, and inspiring quotes my beloved dad wrote to me is in a letter dated March 9, 1989. To this day, his wise words continue to resonate deep within my soul: "It's time to finish what God called you to do. He gives commands. If he has spoken to you to do something, which he has, then do it. No excuses. Find a way. Believe for a miracle. Press on till you win. *Don't quit!*"

Additionally, I have been inspired by the words of motivational guru, Jim Rohn. His encouraging, inspirational, and thought-provoking quotes include:

- "We must all suffer one of two things: the pain of discipline or the pain of regret."
- "Don't wish it was easier, wish you were better. Don't wish for less problems, wish for more skills. Don't wish for less challenge, wish for more wisdom."
- "Discipline is the bridge between goals and accomplishment."
- "Motivation is what gets you started. Habit is what keeps you going."[1]

Two quotes from the great poet Maya Angelou also inspire me on a daily basis:

- "Nothing will work unless you do."
- "All great achievements require time."[2]

I urge you to find the affirmations and quotes that have meaning for you as you do the prep work necessary to create a plan and put it into action with fierce determination to win by reclaiming your health. You are ready to move forward with a mindset of winning with a purpose. Today you have chosen complete ownership of your life.

KEEP THE SELF-CARE FORMULA TOP OF MIND

The critical factor to winning is to keep your actions simple, attainable, and straightforward. Every day you must intentionally work toward your goals. Use the formula we have discussed to guide you:

Fierce Determination + Laser-Focused Actions + Bottomless Discipline
= Deep Beauty and Inner Worth

Putting this formula to work starts first thing in the morning every day when the alarm goes off. What do you choose to do when you hear the alarm clock ringing? Do you just lie there in the comfort of your warm bed when you know you have appointments? Do you just go back to sleep and say, "To heck with it"?

Think about this for a moment. People tell me they don't have time to work out, practice meditation, or eat well because they are too busy. Guess what? If you think you don't have the time, then create it. There are no excuses. If it means getting your butt out of bed early, then take action and get your butt out of bed.

Always remember, discipline is your personal will to succeed. Thrive to learn something new every day. Study and practice your craft. And master it. Your bottomless discipline will transform into greater elements in all areas of your life.

To maintain bottomless discipline in every level in your life, be aware that discipline is not easy. It takes practice, practice, and practice—every day. Then your discipline will start becoming easier because it will be a prominent part of your life and your new habits.

YOUR SEVEN-STEP PLAN

As we discussed earlier, research shows that having a tactical plan reduces anxiety and increases your ability to succeed. Start right now by thinking about what you need to do, using this seven-step process.

Step 1: Define Your Mission

You must see the big picture of the future you want to create in order to own it and win. Be clear, precise, and honest with yourself as to what you really want to accomplish. Ask yourself these kinds of questions to get specific:

- What type of health benefits are you working toward? What about mental health benefits and goals?
- Are you trying to lose weight? Get in better shape? Build strength or flexibility?
- Are you trying to break bad habits?
- Are you striving to increase your chances of living longer and better?
- Are you addressing some physical or mental issues that require medical attention you've been putting off?

Step 2: Prioritize and Analyze Your Needs

Only you know what is on your plate and what you need to make self-care work. Here are some things to do to better understand your needs and priorities.

- Write your list of the projects you are working on for your health.
- Identify the level of importance of each one versus the flexibility you need.
- Evaluate cost and look at options like free meet-up fitness groups.
- Prioritize your tasks by estimated time and effort involved.

Step 3: Create Your Plan

Creating your own self-care plan requires knowledge as well as an understanding that a good plan is comprehensive and integrated. Adding exercise without looking at what you eat will not work. Leaving out a reflective component like meditation that nourishes your soul will not keep you in balance. Here are actions to consider in creating your plan:

- Create realistic goals and expectations. Start with the small steps that will add up to big payoffs later.
- Commit to taking a one-step-at-a-time approach by mastering what you are doing and then moving forward.
- Select only trusted healthcare professionals, mental health professionals, certified trainers, and dietitians to assist you.
- Learn the importance and the benefits of knowing about your immune system, blood type, and body type (chapters 8, 9, 10).

- Learn why your digestive system knows best before you can create your custom lifestyle meal plans (chapter 10).
- Learn to exercise by working around physical challenges and/or disabilities (chapter 11).
- Incorporate "me" time: self-reflection and recovery time.
- Refine your plan as often as you need as you master tasks and learn better what you need to thrive.
- Keep track of your successes, even the small ones.

Step 4: Follow Your Plan

My clients have been clear about what keeps them going. Here are some tips they have shared that resonate with me:

- Keep your daily actions simple.
- Achieve one goal at a time step-by-step.
- Never overload your schedule.
- Know when to stop. Never overtask yourself.
- Understand everything is a process and takes time.
- Take responsibility for your actions.

Step 5: Overcome Challenges

There are two things I know unequivocally. First, practicing self-care will change your life in ways you cannot even begin to imagine. Second, it is a challenging journey. That means you need to plan for challenges. Here are three things you need to plan for:

1. You might get discouraged because you are not seeing results at first. What strategies do you have to counteract discouragement? Talk to a friend? Revisit your mission? Meditate on patience?
2. You may stop for a couple of days because of something in your life. Start back over quickly. The more time you let lapse, the harder it will be.
3. Your partner or family might not be supportive. Do not let this stop you. You are your own true love. They don't need to join you, but they shouldn't stand in your way either.

Step 6: Visualize Daily

What we see, we believe. Visualization is your friend, and you need to practice it daily. Here is how:

- Walk into a room where there is a mirror, preferably a full-length mirror.
- Now take a close look at yourself. Yes, all of you—the beautiful person standing there.
- Meet your new wellness leader. That is the person who will be with you 24/7/365 days of the year to help take you to your victory.
- Understand that every day, you are accountable to that person you see in the mirror.
- Know that you are your only competition. And you are the only one who can get in your way. If you cheat, you are only cheating yourself.
- Tell that person in the mirror that you plan to win, win, and win.
- Every day, know that you are transforming your life through self-care and tapping into your deep beauty and inner worth.

Step 7: Embrace Your Spiritual Connection

Of the thousands of people I have worked with, the ones who were able to achieve and sustain success went beyond the physical aspects of self-care. They had a solid spiritual connection. Some achieved it through meditation. Others were connected to their faith community. Many combined multiple practices. Here are some recommendations to put into your plan:

- Practice your spiritual connection and beliefs daily.
- Practice mindful meditation, yoga, tai chi, and or other mental/physical exercises for strengthening your mind, body, and soul (chapter 13).
- Practice energy healing. Knowing the path is different from walking the path.

"RECLAIMING YOUR HEALTH" QUESTIONS

This is what I would like you to do right now. Sit down for the next hour or so and write down the answers to the following questions. Remember, your answers will be the foundation and the root of your successful health, wellness, and lifestyle journey.

1. Have you seriously made the commitment to reclaiming your health? If so, when did you make the commitment? And how do you plan to follow through with your commitment with your actions? List them.
2. Have you checked with a trusted healthcare professional, certified fitness coach, and/or mentors to assist you? If so, who are they and what is your action plan?

3. What do you think about your new wellness and fitness partner? You know, that beautiful person you met when you looked in the mirror. Are you willing to be accountable to that person? List your actions of accountability.

4. When did you get your "I can do this" attitude or aha moment about reclaiming your health? Describe it.

5. Are you ready to let go of past hurts? If not, why? And have you requested the advice from a credentialed healthcare professional to assist you in this area?

6. List your five favorite daily affirmations. And are you willing to say them daily? If not, why?

7. Do you see a vision of a new healthier you yet? What do you see?

8. Do you have a support system? If not, create and then list your support team. Remember to ask for help by people who are credentialed and have a proven track record of success in reclaiming their health.

9. Are you excited about starting your new wellness journey? What's exciting about it?

10. Are you ready to write down your plan? When will you finish it?

· 6 ·

What Really Happens as We Age

$\mathcal{N}$owadays people are living longer, with the expectations of living a healthier and more vigorous life. Modern technology helps sets these expectations by the advances in medicine as well as the multibillion-dollar cosmetic, fitness, and supplements markets.

Additionally, we live in a new world that is obsessed with finding and keeping the fountain of youth at all cost. Vanity and the obsession of maintaining a youthful appearance cut across all ethnic groups, ages, and genders around the world. Both men and women are willing to spend outrageous sums of money to undergo cosmetic surgeries such as facelifts, skin reduction, tummy tucks, liposuction, breast enhancement, butt lifts, Botox, and so on.

What most people don't understand, however, is that they can discover their own fountain of youth, vitality, energy, and beauty as a side effect of having good health. The real treasure of aging well is to embrace aging head on and not give yourself any excuses. Every day get up, get out, and keep on moving, exercising, meditating, having a positive attitude, and eating foods that are bursting full of antioxidants. All of these treasures will help assist you as you age.

I am not suggesting that anything is wrong with elective surgery for beauty enhancement. But what I am saying is that no operation can help you maintain your youthful appearance as well as transforming your life through self-care. Tapping into your deep beauty and inner worth and learning all you can about self-care will, in fact, help sustain your beauty as you age.

Of course, what happens as we age varies from one person to the next. But the commonality is that it starts with understanding the aging process. Before we examine the science behind what happens as we age, I would like to take a moment and share with you some real talk: my reality of the aging process and the slight telltale physical signs and changes I noticed in myself over time. My story could be your story.

HOW I HAVE AGED

I have always cared about how I look. Long before I understood the deep beauty that comes from within, I was focused on external beauty. So in many ways, I was like other people who can be lured to cosmetic surgery to try to reverse the natural aging process.

When I was sixteen, I noticed my first strand of gray hair. My first thought was, "Oh my goodness, gray hair? Not on my head." I pulled it out immediately. By twenty-eight, I started noticing my hairline thinning around my temple area.

Ten years later, I saw the first wrinkle on my face in a photograph. I thought, "Is that really me? Maybe there is something wrong with the lens of the camera?" Yes, I was somewhat in denial. However, after taking a closer look at myself in the mirror, I acknowledged that the wrinkle on my face in the photograph was indeed real.

As I got closer to forty, I noticed losing weight was not as simple as it once had been. In my twenties, I could skip a meal or two and shed a couple of pounds overnight to fit into that little black cocktail dress. Now I realized skipping a meal to lose weight no longer worked; plus, it depleted my energy. So I started intentionally working harder at how I exercised and what I ate. I became fiercely determined to preserve my beauty. For me, the badge of being a beautiful woman was important to my image and confidence.

Then my focus turned more inward to ways my body was changing. In my early fifties, I started experiencing the symptoms of perimenopause, which forced me to learn self-care strategies for hot flashes and night sweats. During that same time, I began wearing reading glasses. These were all telltale signs that aging had finally caught up with me.

Additionally, my frantic lifestyle and family medical history became concerns. I have already relayed how not taking care of a foot injury, working too hard at my job, and the intense stress of being my father's caregiver almost put me in a wheelchair permanently. I also became very aware that I was approaching an age where multiple family members had died because of heart disease. I am talking in their fifties, not later in life. Was I going to succumb to the same fate? Not if I could help it.

The aging process had my full-blown attention. So I started practicing body building at fifty-four. For my sixtieth birthday present to myself, I took my body to another level of fitness and won first place in the NPC

Women's Figure Championship in the Age 60 and over category. It was a remarkable moment in my life that I experienced by practicing the principles in this book.

Why do I share my story? Because today I have a great appreciation and respect for good health and aging gracefully, but I, like many of you, was not always in that place. Now I cherish every moment of my life and look at each day as a blessing. It's just that straightforward, and anyone can do it.

This is what I know. Everything you do or don't do over a lifetime will add up. Trust me. There will be a day when you recognize everything you've ever done or have not done over your lifetime catches up with you. Your name will be on it because *you are the owner of your health.*

I've had countless discussions with many people of all ages about their personal experiences regarding the aging process. My conclusion is that we should start teaching our children as early as possible about the beauty of aging fearlessly and gracefully by taking healthy actions with self-care. Noticing the slight physical changes in your body as you age enables you to develop a positive mindset early about aging. The importance of taking action by practicing healthy self-care habits early just cannot be underrated.

However, I want to stress that regardless of your age, it's never too late to start. Numerous studies have shown that changing lifestyle habits in terms of diet and exercise, along with quitting smoking, have significant benefits as you grow older, even if you are already getting your AARP card. Before I discuss this research and what you can do, let's take a quick look at the science of aging.

THE SCIENCE OF AGING

I love this informative and funny list that appeared in an article titled "Aging Casefully: 9 Things That Happen to Your Body (Some Aren't So Bad!)." Drawing on science and research, the author, Scott LaFee, shares these things that happen when you age.

1. You sweat less. Well, to be precise, you sweat differently, particularly if you're a woman. Part of the change is related to menopause, i.e. hot flashes, but researchers have found that sweat glands (especially under the arms) shrink and become less sensitive as we age, which translates into reduced perspiration production.
2. You're less buff. Muscle mass in both men and women begins to decline as early as one's 30s, replaced by—gasp!—flab. By age 75, the average person's fat content is twice that of their youth.

3. Your teeth are less sensitive—and not just because you might have fewer of them. The reason is that over time more dentin—the hard inner tissue—is built up between the outer enamel of a tooth and its central nerve. The added insulation diminishes sensitivity. The bad news, though, is that our gums recede over time, exposing roots a different way.

4. Your brain is smaller. As you get older, certain parts of the brain shrink, most notably the prefrontal cortex and hippocampus, both important to learning, memory, planning and other complex mental activities. It's been estimated that the brain begins losing neurons at a rate of 50,000 per day after age 30—more if you listen to certain politicians. But not to fret. For one thing, the average human brain contains more than 100 billion neurons and research has shown that aging brains learn quite well how to adapt. That wizened brain of yours is also likely to be wise beyond its years.

5. You catch fewer colds. This is the payoff for all those years of sneezing, coughing, and runny noses as a kid. By the time you reach middle age, you've been exposed to a diverse host of viruses and have built up a pretty expansive immune response. Been there, caught that.

6. You get fewer migraines (if you're a woman). If hot flashes are the "personal summer bummer" of menopause, the upside is fewer migraines. Research suggests that 67 percent of female migraine sufferers get permanent relief after menopause due to changes in hormone levels.

7. You have less taste. Maybe not in things like clothes (though that might be a matter of debate), but where it literally counts. By age 60, most people have lost half of their taste buds, which research has found is a big reason why older people often compensate by eating more foods high in tasty sugar, salt, and fat.

8. You don't hear so well, either. Hearing loss can begin as early as one's 20s, but tends to be gradual and not really noticeable until your 50s. One in every three adults experiences hearing loss by age 65. By age 75, it's one in two.

9. You get happier. It seems counter-intuitive, but studies show people get happier over time. It's a U-shaped curve. As kids, we generally feel quite good about life, but that sense of well-being diminishes with passing years. Middle age is the nadir, that proverbial time of crisis. But things look up after that.[1]

Humor aside, aging is essentially the gradual but steady erosion of your organ system and your body's built-in capacity to repair itself. That's why you see the outside changes in your hair, teeth, and skin, and the inside changes to your bones, muscles, heart, and lungs. Aging is inevitable, but in the absence of disease, people can live rich lives until they die if they keep their bodies in good working order.

As Dr. Mark Williams explains, "Eventually the body reaches a critical point, usually in very advanced age, when minor problems cannot be overcome and result in the person's death in a relatively short time. For example, a urinary tract infection is usually just a nuisance to a college student but may be the harbinger of serious decline in an 85-year-old person. Consequently, a healthy person who is aging normally will often experience serious illness and weakening only in the last period of life. Exceptions to this ideal aging process are typically the result of diseases such as heart disease or cancer."[2]

One of the things that people often notice as they age is loss of muscle and weaker bones. That's one reason why even the best athletes who studiously practice self-care often need to retire before they are mentally ready. According to the National Institute of Arthritis and Musculoskeletal and Skin Diseases, the majority of people will lose a substantial amount of muscle as they age. Additionally, bones start to thin, become more porous, and grow slower. These changes occur differently in each individual, but they will affect everyone. And some ethnic groups can be particularly vulnerable. For example, studies show that Asian American women are at the highest risk of developing bone loss osteoporosis.[3]

For many people, one of the scariest things about aging is changes in their memory and ability to learn new things. You may be getting wiser, I hope, but some brain functions do change. For example, research indicates that learning new things and memorizing new information takes longer and can be more difficult. Multitasking is harder because your brain processes information slower. Remembering names and numbers actually starts declining at age twenty. Fortunately, there are exercises to keep your brain working better and many technological tools to help you when your own storage of information is not accessible.[4]

But some people don't experience aging like the majority of us do. They are called super-agers, individuals over the age of eighty whose mental and physical abilities far exceed their peers of the same age.

LEARN FROM THE SUPER-AGERS

My friend Goldine is one of my favorite super-agers. At eighty, Goldine has the body of a women's figure champion and the memory of someone half her age. I asked her to share her secret of aging well. She said,

> Carolyn, I had to reprogram my brain and start thinking differently. For example, I made my mind up that my eightieth birthday present to myself

was to lose the twenty pounds I had packed on over the years. I was determined to fit into the expensive clothes that were hanging in my closet. I stopped smoking nearly twenty years ago, and if I could do that, I can do anything I set in my mind to do.

Super-agers are under the scrutiny of many scientists and medical researchers to help understand and even help reverse conditions that come with aging. For example, super-agers' brains shrink at a slower rate than other people their age. They are more resistant to memory loss and enjoy their later years in life. Using MRIs, researchers actually found a difference in the physical construction of the brain of super-agers. They have a thicker cortex than those who age normally. This finding may lead researchers to better understand how to reduce cortical brain atrophy that contributes to lost memory ability as we age.[5]

At Harvard University, researchers have been tracking a group of individuals for eighty years, one of the longest studies ever done. Researchers there found that the one factor that plays a big role in longevity is social interaction, specifically relationships. People who lived longer had very close relationships over the years.[6]

There have also been some surprising findings about diet and exercise habits and how they affect ninety-somethings and above. The 90+ Study was initiated in 2003 to study the oldest-old, the fastest growing age group in the United States. More than 1,600 people have enrolled. Participants in the 90+ Study are visited every six months by researchers who give cognitive and physical tests as well as ask questions about diet, activities, medical history, medications, and numerous other factors.

This work is the first to show an association between exercising at age sixty through one's seventies and a lower risk of falling at age ninety and above. Additionally, there were two fascinating findings about diet: (1) people who drank moderate amounts of alcohol or coffee lived longer than those who abstained and (2) people who were overweight in their seventies lived longer than normal or underweight people did.[7]

You've seen some interesting research on factors such as exercise, relationships, alcohol, and caffeine. Now let's take a broader look at food.

TAPPING INTO ANTI-AGING SUPERFOODS

Numerous studies have found that a predominantly plant-based diet can help to decrease the risk of obesity, diabetes, heart disease, and overall mortality. There is also quite a bit of evidence that there are superfoods that combat aging. I will be talking about diet extensively later in this book, but for now

I want you to remember that good health starts in the kitchen because you are what you eat. Here are seven superfoods to consider adding to your diet.

1. Fish oil or cold water fish. These foods contain high levels of omega-3s, which improve the body's ability to convert fat to energy during exercise, reduce insulin levels, block fat storage in the body, and reduce cortisol, a stress-related hormone that causes fat storage in the body.
2. Olive oil. Studies show that people eating two tablespoons of virgin, organic olive oil daily for one week show less oxidation of LDLs and higher levels of antioxidants in their blood.[8]
3. Avocados. Avocados contain twenty-five milligrams per ounce of a natural plant sterol called beta-sitosterol, which can help maintain healthy cholesterol levels. Half of an avocado provides approximately 25 percent of the daily recommended intake of vitamin K, which is essential for bone health. An avocado is actually high in fiber with approximately six to seven grams per half fruit.
4. Blueberries. Blueberries are high in antioxidants, help fight cancer, amp up weight loss, boost brain health, alleviate inflammation, support digestion, and promote heart health.
5. Watercress. Watercress decreases the risk of obesity, diabetes, heart disease, and overall mortality while promoting a healthy complexion, increased energy, and overall lower weight.
6. Walnuts. Walnuts are high in protein, vitamins, omega-3 fatty acids, trace minerals, lecithin, and oils. Walnuts are unique because the fats in them are primarily polyunsaturated fatty acids. Moreover, walnuts have insignificant amounts of sodium and are cholesterol-free.
7. Garlic. Garlic protects against cell damage and aging, helps reduce cholesterol and blood pressure, and may help prevent Alzheimer's disease and dementia.

YOUR DAILY AGING WITH GRACE CHECKLIST

So what is the bottom line about how to age well, now that you understand what happens when you age? Based on research, my own experience, and working with clients, here's my Lucky 13 list:

1. Drink more water.
2. Ban sugar from your diet.
3. Eat more nutritious good fats.
4. Aim for a gluten-free lifestyle.

5. Reduce stress as much as possible.
6. Increase your intake of antioxidants.
7. Eat more foods rich in protein.
8. Exercise and lift more weights.
9. Mindfully meditate.
10. Incorporate more natural beauty products.
11. Get plenty of sleep, and take naps when you are tired.
12. Go and have a little fun.
13. Cherish every moment of your life.

Practicing the items on this list on a daily basis requires discipline. It is very easy to get distracted from a self-care plan. In the next chapter, I will explore why discipline is so important. So keep on reading.

"WHAT REALLY HAPPENS AS WE AGE" QUESTIONS

Think about your views regarding aging. In your personal binder, start writing your thoughts and answer the following questions:

1. What are your true feelings about aging? Do you fear growing old? If so, why?
2. At what age were you when you first noticed signs of aging? What were the signs? And what were your reactions?
3. What are your thoughts about maintaining a youthful appearance?
4. What are your thoughts about the benefits of aging?
5. What actions are you taking to help slow down the aging process?
6. Which antiaging superfoods are already in your kitchen? If you do not have any, then which ones are you going to purchase?
7. Which self-care best practices are you willing to commit to in order to feel and look your best as you age?
8. Can you see yourself becoming a super-ager? If not, why not?

· 7 ·

Why Discipline Is Important

$\mathscr{D}$iscipline is not a very popular word in our culture. In fact, sometimes it seems like it is almost a dirty word. In our schools, parents often side with their children instead of teachers when Johnny acts out in class or doesn't complete homework. In workplaces, one of the most persistent complaints around employees is that they lack discipline and don't work hard. The list goes on and on as people blame bad judgment, behavior, and choices on other people or circumstances; the individual who's acting out is too often not held accountable.

This mindset is particularly harmful when it comes to self-care. We join health clubs in January and after a few months rarely go back. We are lured by instant gratification when it comes to fast food that we know is not healthy for us. We indulge in behavior that hurts our relationships, families, and, most importantly, ourselves.

Here, however, is the simple truth: You cannot transform your life if you don't do the hard work every single day. That calls for discipline. And here's another observation: The more you practice discipline in your life and see the rewards, the more you will yearn for it. You will increase your sense of worthiness and get results. That is what's in it for you.

Having discipline is the core foundation and structure that will benefit you in every area of your life. Whether it is emotional or physical, it all boils down to self-discipline. Just know that when you surrender to intentionally practicing bottomless discipline, you will create the solid-rock foundation you can count on when you are working toward achieving any goal.

Where do you start? First, you must know specifically what it is that you want. Once you know what you want, then you will be ready to press the reset button on your life and shift your thoughts to a brand-new paradigm. Then you must be committed to going after what it is you want to accomplish.

57

Are you willing to do what it takes for you to succeed? Are you willing to commit your time? Are you aware that you may have to acquire additional education? Are you up to reading more books? Are you willing to upgrade your skills or seek professional guidance? When you genuinely want to succeed, you will do what it takes. You will not allow anything to stop you. You will honor yourself and keep your commitments. And you will tell yourself that no excuse is acceptable.

Just remember one thing: Greatness takes time, and you've got to be hungry enough to work your plan and never give up. I assure you that once you know what you want and commit to doing the work, the genius in you—the God-given talents and gifts that you were born with—will indeed assist you every step of the way to creating your new life.

The process of discipline starts with the mind. Everything we do and don't do starts with a thought. And too often, mental toxins can get in the way.

DISCIPLINING YOUR MIND

Let's keep it simple: What is the difference between the mind and the brain? The mind is the driver of input, thought, and actions, which are the consciousness, education, and the driver of discipline. The brain is the organ in which neurotransmitters shuttle messages between cells. The mind and the brain must be working purposely together to achieve the discipline that will help you reach your goals. Case in point, if the brain is dead, the mind cannot function. Likewise, if the mind is full of mental toxins, you cannot feed your brain the stimuli it needs to flourish.

Let's take a closer look at what scientists have to say about how the brain delivers messages in our body. According to Dr. Bethany Brookshire, a science journalist for *Science News for Students*, "Neurotransmitters shuttle messages between cells. Every time a nerve needs to make a muscle move, it releases a burst of neurotransmitters."

A neurotransmitter is a chemical that serves as a message from one cell to another. When a brain cell needs to pass a signal to a neighbor, it releases a tiny cloud called a neurotransmitter, which floats across the space between two cells and binds to proteins called receptors on the next cell. The receptors pass along those signals, which tells the cells what they are being "asked to do."[1]

The mind needs detoxing just like the body needs detoxing. It is impossible to achieve the greatness of transforming your life through self-care if you do not have the discipline to detox your mind. Your mind is where it all begins, and you are the CEO and order-giver to every part of your body from the crown of your head to the bottom of your feet. When you have discipline over your thoughts, you allow your mind to flourish.

Yes, you have the power to detox your mind. To achieve this, it is necessary to develop a made-up mind and ban all toxic, negative thoughts of fear, laziness, doubt, anger, hopelessness, envy, greed, self-pity, and any other undesirable form of stinking thinking.

Think about it. Every day we are bombarded with the latest breaking news stories, which seem to guarantee to deliver bad news. Let's face it: Bad news sells. However, imagine if the latest toxic news story is your "mental meal" diet plan for life? How toxic do you think your mind will become? Over time, when you are continually feeding yourself an overdose of daily bad news, *mental toxins* will eventually kill your spirit.

When you find yourself struggling with toxic and destructive thoughts, redirect those negative feelings. You have the power to change what you are thinking and create a new mindset to think about things that will inspire and soothe your soul. Incorporate activities of relaxation for your mind, body, and spirit. Go for a walk. Practice meditation. Go for a good workout. Take a therapeutic bubble bath. Just be in the moment of focusing on having a healthy detoxed mind and renewing of your soul.

DISCIPLINING YOUR TONGUE

Have you thought about how to discipline your tongue? The tongue is the body part that controls everything we say or don't say and eat or don't eat. The tongue can be the most challenging body part to discipline, for the words it speaks can be nefarious, benefiting no one.

As I mentioned in the introduction—but it doesn't hurt to repeat it as a reminder—the words you speak are essential. They can inspire or deflate, ignite or extinguish, drive you to action or move you to despair.

The words others use against us have power. However, the words we use against ourselves are infinitely more powerful: "I am not worth it." "I can't." "I give up." We have all used those words against ourselves at some point in our lives, and the results can be devastating.

I'd like to share with you a story about how powerful the tongue is, as reflected in the words you speak. John and JoAnn were avid bicycle riders in a local bike-riding club in San Francisco, where the hills are very steep. JoAnn always had an issue with riding up the steep hills. She consistently said, "I can't ride up steep hills," although she had never tried climbing up a hill on her bicycle before. John encouraged JoAnn to speak positive words and start believing that riding up an elevation was not a big deal.

On their next ride, JoAnn successfully climbed up the steep hill because she told herself that the slope was not a big deal. As she began pedaling, she spoke words of power by saying, "I can climb this hill, and it's not a big deal." She made it to the top of the hill.

JoAnn's success came from speaking the powerful words of "I can," which gave her confidence. "Yes, I can." "I can do it." "I am strong." "I believe." Yes, there is power in the tongue, which must be disciplined when you speak.

Additionally, the tongue controls foods we crave, where our taste buds tell us what and how much to eat. Unless you take control over your tongue, it has the power to get out of control and lead you to develop numerous addictions and cravings. In short, the tongue can be your best friend or your worst enemy.

Often, the tongue has the power to ultimately rule over what comes in and out of your mouth. Sometimes, the tongue can leave a person fighting with himself or herself: The battle is between what the mind thinks and what the tongue speaks and/or eats. How can something so small control us the way the tongue does? Have you thought about how to discipline your tongue?

DISCIPLINING EMOTIONS

Emotional control will help you in every area of your life. Emotional discipline demonstrates acts of kindness in the midst of a storm: when you are arguing with your partner or love interest, when you are stuck in traffic and someone cuts you off while you are driving, when you at the grocery store or a restaurant and you are not happy with the customer service, or when you are sitting in a boring meeting at work and you want to leave but can't.

Developing emotional discipline is not the simplest thing to do and will require practicing patience. Sometimes you may find yourself just walking away from a situation to avoid conflict. Perhaps the more spiritual way to safeguard your heart is by taking the high road.

Emotional discipline will test you when you want to say the wrong thing but are disciplined enough to say and do the right thing. A perfect example was how I handled Liam and his mistress (chapter 2). Trust me, it wasn't easy for me to keep my cool for the first twenty-four hours after I found out that Liam was having an affair. In that case, I used emotional discipline to maintain the wisdom to bridle my tongue from the words that were swirling around in my head. Because I applied emotional discipline, it helped remove me from a negative situation and be safe.

Keep in mind that emotional discipline starts first thing in the morning, when you wake up. That is when you create the opportunity to set the standard for your day, by saying, "I am happy, I am blessed, I am joyful, I am alive, and nothing will stop me from embracing this day."

Occasionally our feelings can overtake us, but there are steps we can take to overcome them. By shifting the way you see something, it's possible to turn obstacles into breakthroughs for success. According to Hara Estroff Marano, creator of *Psychology Today*'s *Blues Buster* newsletter, you can choose any of a number of strategies to work with your feelings. Here are two of the most essential and effective ones that you can access through your mind.[2]

- Mental Reframing: By changing the way you see something, it's possible to turn setbacks into opportunities for success. When you find yourself in a difficult emotional situation, focus on the opportunities in it as well as the risks. An argument, for example, provides a chance to learn something about relationships and the different ways people see things.
- Emotional Kung Fu: In the Chinese art of self-defense known as kung fu, the aim is to use any attacking force to your advantage. You don't fight the attacker; you redirect their energy to accomplish your goal.

DISCIPLINING YOUR BODY

When I was fifty-four years old, I took a real close look in the mirror for the very first time. Yes, I looked directly into my eyes and started examining what I was feeling deep within my soul. In fact, I was studying and tapping into my deep beauty and inner worth. By that time, I had already worked a lot on clearing my mind and embracing my spirit. Now I was ready to make physical discipline a top priority as well.

I was ready to start living in the present moment by intentionally making a difference in my physical health, starting from the inside out. I recognized I had a lot of hard work to do, and I loved myself enough to do everything necessary to make a difference in my life. Physically, my body was falling apart bit by bit before my very eyes, and I was in constant pain. I knew it was up to me to make the difference in my life.

Although I had a pharmaceutical background, I knew I did not want opioids to be my first-line pain treatment; I didn't want to be that lady who walks into the doctor's office with a bag full of pills. No, that was not going to be me. Instead, I chose the medicinal route toward self-healing, and I recognized that eating foods bursting full of antioxidants and using other therapeutic techniques would be my first-line choice. I understood it was up to me to change my physical health and well-being by applying the necessary discipline.

As I began the process of rebuilding my body, I searched for medical healthcare professionals and certified fitness coaches that had similar healthcare visions as I did, to help me achieve success with my overall fitness goals.

One of the first things I thought about was a natural body-builder fitness group. I believe that whatever you are searching for, you should go directly to the experts and learn from the best. They will show you how to be a winner and will be by your side every step of the way. I will forever be grateful to my fitness coach, Jocelyn Jean, International Federation of Bodybuilding and Fitness (IFBB) Pro Bodybuilder.

First, Jocelyn had me study and practice the habits and the mindset of body builders. Wow, these folks are the most disciplined group of people I have ever met in my life. I was then and I am now still fascinated by the fierce discipline, structure, and determination body builders must have to be the best of the best.

In addition, Jocelyn had me study the different meal plans and exercises for each fitness group, whether body builders, bikini division, or women's figure champions. He wanted me to understand that they all had one common characteristic: physical discipline with fierce determination to win.

For months, body-builder athletes are committed to transforming their bodies in preparation for show time. Getting up on stage for the first time in a body-building competition is indeed not an easy task. Often, the onstage performance is less than five minutes of flexing.

The work was hard initially. I lost twenty pounds of fat and turned it into solid muscle. However, over time my body achieved the deep discipline that helped me to win, breaking old habits and creating new and healthy habits. I competed and won.

I encourage you to attend a body-building competition, to be in the audience and listen to some of the beautiful stories from competitors on stage. Some have beaten the odds of sickness and diseases such as cancer, diabetes, heart disease, hypertension, high blood cholesterol, and more.

At this point, I hope you have a better understanding of why discipline is important and how it works. This chapter has discussed both the emotional and physical aspects of discipline. Now let's focus purely on the physical with an important discussion of how your circulatory and immune systems work.

"WHY DISCIPLINE IS IMPORTANT" QUESTIONS

Now it's time to pull out your binder or computer and act on recognizing the importance of discipline:

1. What areas of discipline do you need to start working on?
2. Do you see the emotional and physical benefits of having discipline?
3. Are you committed to going after what it is you want to accomplish? What are you committed to do?
4. What are your thoughts about detoxing your mind? And what actions will you take for enlightening that will provide you clearing of the mind?
5. What areas of concern do you have regarding your emotional discipline?
6. What will be the most challenging part about disciplining your tongue regarding what goes in your mouth and the powerful words that you speak?

· 8 ·

Blood Types and Your Immune System

$\mathcal{W}$e don't often talk about the nitty-gritty stuff that keeps our bodies healthy, like understanding our blood type and immune system. Until you donate blood or go in for surgery, chances are you probably don't even know your blood type. Until you suffer a disease that attacks your immune system, you probably just don't think about this vital function.

In fact, for many years even the medical community was not focused on diseases that attack the immune system. For example, lupus, an autoimmune disease, was pretty much ignored until about thirty years ago, even though 1.5 million Americans and more than five million people worldwide suffer from the devastating consequences of this illness. For years, women—who make up 90 percent of the sufferers—had their symptoms dismissed and were told, "It's all in your head."[1]

And while there is growing interest in blood types in terms of diets and connection with diseases, there is not a substantial amount of evidence-based research to back up many theories. One exception is a recent study at the Harvard School of Public Health that found that people with blood types A, B, or AB have a higher risk for coronary heart disease than people with blood type O. Those with the rarest blood type, AB, had the greatest risk.[2]

Having this information can help motivate people with a certain blood type to take better preventive measures. Researchers are now calling for more studies to examine the relationship between blood types, disease, and nutrition. Additionally, recent advances in medical technology and measurement are opening up better ways to study this field.

So you may watch your weight, worry about cholesterol, and control high blood pressure, but if you are like most people, you don't really pay attention to either understanding or taking actions on two of the most vital aspects of your health—blood type and the immune system. After reading this chapter, hopefully you will.

A SELF-CARE PATH GONE
WRONG AND THEN RIGHT

I'd like to start by sharing my own story and what ignited my desire to learn more about how blood types and the immune system work. My story is also a lesson in why it is so important to always check with healthcare professionals before starting any new diet, cleansing, and or weight loss programs.

I spent many years of my career in the pharmaceutical industry, with a great deal of travel. During one trip to New Jersey from California, my company supplied the housing, food, and transportation for over five hundred people who attended the long training. All of the meals were prepared in bulk with a setup very similar to the way food is displayed on a cruise ship.

After a couple of days of eating buffet-style meals, I began feeling sick to my stomach. I decided to meet with the onsite company staff nurse about my sudden stomach pain, severe bloating, and feelings of nausea. She could not find a cause and recommended that I stay hydrated, eat very light foods, and take antacids for the rest of the training.

Those measures did not help. I continued feeling nauseated only after eating meals, which eventually I quit doing altogether. The day finally came when my four-week training program was over. While I was in New Jersey, I had gained fifteen pounds even though I was eating soups, salads, and then nothing.

Back home, my doctor ran every blood test imaginable on me. Additionally, he ordered a CT angiograph, a scan that injects a contrast dye that highlights blood vessels and tissues in the abdomen, to determine the cause of my stomach pain, nausea, bloating, water retention, and weight gain.

A few days later, I followed up with my doctor. He said, "Carolyn, I have some good news and not so good news for you. Which would you like to hear first?"

"Please tell me the bad news first," I said.

"Carolyn, your immune system is highly sensitive and allergic to excessive amounts of pesticides, nitrites, sulfides, preservatives, hormones, food dyes, and all genetically modified engineered foods. It appears that your body reacted to the foods you were eating as poisons. That is the bad news. However, the good news is that now you know this crucial information, you can look at this as an opportunity to become healthier. When you start eating the right foods for your body, you will start feeling better. I suggest that you learn more about certified organic, non–genetically modified foods."

I had a new profound awakening: Today is the beginning of my new life, and health self-care journey. I began dramatically changing my diet and became an avid label reader. I now understood that these substances in food were attacking my body because I was allergic to them. My immune system was then overreacting by producing antibodies to attack the allergens. My symptoms were serious consequences of my immune system's reaction.

A few years later, in 2011, I was a guest on a television show in San Francisco, California, promoting my first book. After the show was over, I had the pleasure of sitting with the show's host, a woman named Janet. I shared my discovery of allergic reaction and how I was learning about nutrition and making food my first-line choice of medicine.

I also commented on her beautiful and vibrant skin and asked what she was using on it. She said, "Thank you, Carolyn, but the radiance you are seeing is coming from inside of my body, and the beauty from within is manifesting the results on my skin."

Janet had been going to the Vegan Health Institute (name changed) and gotten amazing health results. The place specialized in certified organic whole foods and non–genetically modified, vegan health foods. She suggested that I attend in order to jumpstart my own nutritional journey.

On Christmas Day, nearly two weeks before my fifty-fifth birthday, I checked myself into a vegan health and wellness program for one week of cleansing, meditation, and self-healing. This was my Christmas present to myself to detox my body and invest in my health.

Notice I didn't wait until New Year's Day to start my program; that's a classic strategy that so many people use. Starting at the beginning of the year wasn't going to work for me because I'd realized I had already waited long enough. So I didn't wait for a magical date. I just did it. And I was feeling really excited about both what was going to happen and how good I anticipated feeling.

Prior to my week of detoxing my body, I was informed that I might start feeling lethargic while my body was cleansing. I was assured that feeling exhausted was part of the detoxing and healing process, and it would be transient and short-lived.

After seven days, I lost nearly ten pounds, which thrilled me. My blood pressure levels dropped down to a hypotensive state—low blood pressure. I wasn't worried because I thought that my body was healing itself. So I took myself off my prescribed water pills because I thought I no longer need them to manage my high blood pressure.

But the feeling of extreme exhaustion never went away. By pure coincidence, a week later I had my regular quarterly appointment with my cardiologist at the San Francisco University Medical Center. At that time, I was my cardiologist's youngest heart patient due to my family's medical history of heart disease.

As a standard question, my cardiologist asked me, "Carolyn, have you experienced any medical changes since your last visit?" I immediately said, "Since I started my vegan diet, I've lost ten pounds, I'm fatigued, and I stopped taking my water pills due to experiencing hypotension."

She immediately hooked me up to an EKG. The results were that my heart was working harder and was enlarged. I was shocked by the results. My doctor said, "Carolyn, never take yourself off of any medications unless it's medically supervised. You are lucky that you came in when you did; the results could have been much worse if you had waited."

What happened to me reinforced another important lesson that I had forgotten (I don't always learn on the first try): Always check with healthcare professionals before starting any new diet, cleansing, or exercise program. Wow, what a sobering experience that was for me.

My cardiologist also suggested that I look at a food plan that was connected to my blood type. She had done research in this area and seen the results with some of her patients.

Both doctors were telling me the same thing: My health challenges were directly related to the foods I was eating. My immune system is highly sensitive to nitrites, sulfides, preservatives, hormones, food dyes, and genetically modified, engineered foods. The enlargement of my heart occurred by switching to a diet that was not compatible with my body as well as by going off the water pills without supervision.

Quite simply, I had to eat right for *me*. It did not matter if others considered the food healthy. It did not matter if research had shown an additive to be harmless. It did not matter where my own personal taste or even moral leaning took me. I had to eat exactly and precisely *what my body needed*.

I discovered the book *Eat Right for Your Type* by naturopathic physician Peter J. D'Adamo. In the book, Dr. D'Adamo explains a diet plan based upon blood type. He also recommends eating organic food as much as possible and avoiding processed foods and simple carbs.

His theory is that our blood types are a roadmap to our inner chemistry, and each blood type processes food, handles stress, and fights disease differently. Essentially, the foods you eat react chemically with your blood type. Your body will digest food more efficiently if you eat according to your blood type. This will help you have more energy and help prevent disease. Here are his recommendations:

- If you have type O blood, you need a high protein diet of lean meat, poultry, fish, and vegetables. You should eat grains, beans, and dairy sparingly.
- Type A's should eat a meat-free diet of fruits, vegetables, beans, legumes, and whole grains.
- People with type B blood should eat green vegetables, eggs, certain meats, and low-fat dairy. They should avoid corn, wheat, lentils, tomatoes, peanuts, and chicken.
- AB blood types need to focus on tofu, seafood, dairy, and green vegetables and avoid caffeine, alcohol, and smoked meats.[3]

The principles of this book met my health goals, but before I began another wellness dietary journey, I checked with my healthcare professionals first. Once I got the clearance to start my new eating plan, I almost immediately felt more energized, and my digestive system felt much better.

A few years later, when I moved to Florida, I met my new doctor, an internal medicine physician and wellness specialist. She uses cutting-edge technologies and loves helping others thrive and elevate their fitness, vitality, and happiness. Her thoughts were in direct alignment with my wellness goals. She was the perfect healthcare professional to help take me to my next level of wellness without harming myself, as I unknowingly had done years before.

My doctor assisted me in understanding the foods, vitamins, and nutritional supplements that were best for my body and blood type and would also bolster my immune system. Based on my blood type, she suggested that I learn and master the Mediterranean diet. Since complying with her recommendations, my blood tests continue to be outstanding. I am now experiencing the results I had been searching for—although it had taken me years.

There are three lessons I want you to take away from my story:

1. Work in conjunction with healthcare professionals you trust and who know your complete health picture.
2. Don't assume that a certain type of diet is healthy for you, even if it is touted as the healthiest way of eating. As it turned out, a vegan lifestyle does not provide the protein my body needs.
3. Finding the right food plan is a journey. But once you reach your destination, don't play around. Your body needs you to do exactly what it is asking of you.

IS THE BLOOD TYPE DIET LEGITIMATE?

There simply has been very little research done on the blood type diet. As I mentioned before, research on blood types itself is scarce, although it is attracting more interest. This is what Dr. John Briffa, author of *Escape the Diet Trap*, has to say about eating to your blood type: "The fact is, it's not actually been studied properly at all. And, as the saying goes, the absence of evidence is not evidence of absence. If the diet was subjected to proper study, it might turn out to work just as Peter D'Adamo says it does."[4]

Does lack of research about the blood type diet mean that it is a bad idea? I don't think so at all. There are many things that are not researched—particularly in Western medicine—because of biases. For years, acupuncture, organic food, massage, and nutritional supplements were considered outside the mainstream. The medical community did not legitimize them. That is no longer true.

Additionally, medical research, particularly around food, is constantly being reevaluated. Remember when we were scared of eggs because we were told they directly caused high cholesterol? For decades, doctors recommended avoiding high-fat food. Now studies are suggesting that high fat can enhance memory, improve physical strength, and extend your life span.

The point is that medical research is not always right. My view is that the blood type diet makes a tremendous amount of sense. If you chose this path, you would essentially be eating cleaner, and that is vital to good health.

Several of my clients noticed the significant positive changes in my body, health, and spirit as I grew older. They asked me to duplicate the actions I took that changed my quality of life. As such they were testing out the blood type diet.

Here is what I required of each client:

- Get permission from his or her healthcare professional.
- Know his or her blood type and eat foods that were compatible with that blood type.
- Commit to eating only certified, organic whole and non–genetically modified foods.
- Journal all meals daily, including snacks and cheat days.
- Record exercise, if exercising on a daily basis.
- Make a three-month commitment.
- Check in twice a week.

Here are a few stories from their experiences. Nguyen is a twenty-four-year-old woman who felt worn out; she wanted more energy and vitality. She has type O blood. Working full time and attending night school, she has found the diet challenging because it requires time and focus. Additionally, she is young, so eating a midnight snack of brownies and drinking red wine was important to her. She feels that she has achieved great results and has more energy. And she is very aware that on the days she cheats, she does not feel great the next day. The bottom line: Today Nguyen works hard to adhere to a Mediterranean lifestyle diet as much as she can, because she likes feeling energized.

Thell also had type O blood. At seventy-five, she was overweight with severe back and knee pain from arthritis. She could hardly walk. Like Nguyen, she did not find the diet easy to do but was amazed by the results. She lost thirty-five pounds and is considerably more mobile. The bottom line: even though it was difficult, Thell now has regained mobility and is aging gracefully.

Lisa was half of Thell's age and also overweight. Often fatigued, she simply wanted to feel better. A type A, she now eats plenty of fish, including salmon, sea or rainbow trout, red snapper, cod, and mackerel. She's down twenty pounds and feeling great. The bottom line: Lisa never thought about eating food for her blood type but is now convinced that it works.

At sixty-two, William became a vegan because of his AB blood type. He lost twenty-five pounds, no longer has fat around his belly, and is full of energy. The bottom line: He says he hasn't felt this good since he was in his twenties.

These sample stories and my own have me thoroughly convinced that eating for your blood type leads to greater health, vitality, and overall wellness. Our blood tells us what we need and what foods to eat. The only thing we must learn to do is listen to our body.

My recommendation is for you to find out your blood type and put together a test based on the knowledge you get from reading D'Adamo's book. Make sure you use the requirements I asked of my clients.

By the way, in addition to nutritional reasons, it is valuable to know your blood type in case of emergencies or if you are doing international travel. So how can you find out what yours is?

- Donate blood to the Red Cross.
- Order an online blood type testing kit.
- Contact your doctor, who will have the information if you have had surgery or a pregnancy.
- Go directly to a direct access lab. You can order tests from most walk-in labs. There is a high likelihood your insurer will not pay for it, so make sure you find out the cost.

YOUR IMMUNE SYSTEM AND YOUR EATING PLAN

Even if you are eating to your blood type, it is also very important to understand if your body has food intolerances or allergies. If you don't understand that, then you can be eating what seems to be right but still not feeling well.

For example, I fortunately learned about my allergies to pesticides, nitrites, sulfides, preservatives, hormones, food dyes, and all genetically modified, engineered foods before I started eating for my blood type. If I hadn't, the blood type diet would not have worked as well. Most people do not have the level of reaction I do to these substances. I absolutely need to be an avid label reader or I get sick—very sick.

Incidentally, while I have severe allergies, I believe that there are more people who have adverse reactions to these substances than are acknowledged. That's one of the reasons that many nutritional experts recommend eating as clean as possible.

What exactly does that mean? Clean eating means embracing whole foods like vegetables, fruits, and whole grains, plus healthy proteins and fats. It means cutting back on refined grains, additives, preservatives, unhealthy fats, and large amounts of added sugar and salt. It means buying organic as much as possible and avoiding processed foods for which you need a chemistry degree to figure out what the label is saying.

It is my belief that if you do this, then your immune system will not fight against you, because it will be at peace with what you are putting in your body. Again, I urge you to try this and see the results. I think you will be amazed.

But even with clean eating, you need to be aware of personal food intolerances and allergies. A food intolerance is less severe than a food allergy. You may be able to eat problem foods without a reaction—in small quantities. By comparison, eating even a tiny amount of a food that you are allergic to can trigger a severe reaction.

When you have a food allergy, your immune system mistakenly identifies a specific food or a substance in the food as harmful. It responds by releasing an antibody known as immunoglobulin E (IgE) to neutralize the allergy causing food or food substance. The next time you eat even the smallest amount of that food, IgE antibodies sense it and signal your immune system to release a chemical called histamine, as well as other chemicals, into your bloodstream.

Common reactions by your immune system can occur immediately or within a few hours and include:

- Tingling or itching in the mouth
- Hives, itching, or eczema
- Swelling of the lips, face, tongue, and throat or other parts of the body

- Wheezing, nasal congestion, or trouble breathing
- Abdominal pain, diarrhea, nausea, or vomiting
- Dizziness, lightheadedness, or fainting

A severe, life-threatening food allergic reaction called anaphylaxis requires immediate medical attention. Symptoms can include:

- Constriction and tightening of the airways
- A swollen throat or the sensation of a lump in your throat that makes it difficult to breathe
- Shock with a severe drop in blood pressure
- Rapid pulse
- Dizziness, lightheadedness, or loss of consciousness[5]

One client of mine, for example, used to get headaches after certain meals. She finally figured out that it happened after eating her favorite seafood: shrimp. When she had allergy testing done, her allergic reaction to shrimp was significant. But she really didn't want to believe it. So she experimented and found out the truth for herself. Eat shrimp, get a headache. Eat more shrimp, get really sick.

Shellfish are a common source of food intolerance or allergies. In fact, eight things cause about 90 percent of food allergy reactions:

- Milk
- Eggs
- Peanuts
- Tree nuts like walnuts, almonds, and pecans
- Soy
- Wheat and other grains with gluten, including barley, rye, and oats
- Fish
- Shellfish

Less common ones include:

- Corn
- Gelatin
- Meat—beef, chicken, mutton, and pork
- Seeds, often sesame, sunflower, and poppy
- Spices, such as caraway, coriander, garlic, and mustard[6]

So now you have a foundation of how blood types and your immune system relate to what you eat. Let's bridge over to how to improve your wellness by creating your custom meal plan. As you read the next chapter, I believe you will have aha moments that will help you stop the yo-yo diets that you may have experienced for years and find a stable way to gain good health through eating.

"BLOOD TYPES AND YOUR IMMUNE SYSTEM" QUESTIONS

Now it's your time to pull out your binder or computer to answer questions that will help you formulate a food plan through a better understanding of your blood type and immune system.

1. What is your understanding of how your blood type and immune system work? And what is the benefit for you?
2. Do you know your blood type? If so, what is it? If not, when do you plan to get your blood type information?
3. What foods are you allergic to that you know of?
4. Do you ever experience bloating, nausea, headaches, and other symptoms after eating a meal?
5. Have you ever tried eliminating certain foods from your diet to see if you feel better? What was the result?
6. Are you aware of the importance of collaborating with your health-care professional before making any dietary changes—especially if you are on any medications?

· 9 ·

Developing Your Own Meal Plan

*Y*ou now know the importance of understanding any food intolerances and allergies you may have. You also have learned about the idea of clean eating. These are important ideas to keep your immune system balanced. And I have shared in-depth my journey back to health, as well as those of my clients, by eating according to blood type.

Now let's go even deeper into why food choices matter, which foods are best for you, which foods are worst for you, why planning is important, and what suggestions can be made for meal planning. I also want to talk about being overweight. While I personally have not had to deal with being overweight, a significant number of my clients come to me with that issue as their number-one problem. They rightfully believe that changing their eating habits and exercising more will help them lose weight.

However, what they don't understand is that most weight loss efforts are doomed to failure—not because people can't lose weight but rather because they can't keep it off. While there is a lot of debate as to why most people put the weight back on—95 percent is an often-quoted statistic—the point is that at the end of the day it is not about losing weight but rather practicing self-care every day of your life.

I am going to take you through several rules that are essential to food planning. But before we go there, I want to remind you of our self-care formula:

Fierce Determination + Laser-Focused Actions + Bottomless Discipline
= Deep Beauty + Inner Worth

Food planning requires fierce determination. You need to stop at nothing to put into your body the food that it needs to thrive. Forget about time, money, and inconvenience. You need to be fierce in your approach, because that is your road to happiness.

Food planning requires laser-focused actions. Planning in itself is an action. Shopping correctly is an action. Reading labels is an action. Not eating out is an action. All of these actions add up. "Laser-focused" means that your goal is always top of mind. Even when you are making exceptions, you do it intentionally: 'I am going on a vacation for a week. I will allow myself to have . . ." What you may find out, surprisingly, is that sticking to your food plan on vacation actually makes you enjoy your time more, because your body feels great.

Food planning requires bottomless discipline. You live in a world intent on making this hard for you. Advertising, family gatherings, food-focused events, work obligations—they will all challenge you. But you are that Olympic athlete with bottomless discipline.

Finally, these actions take you to a place of deep beauty and inner worth. They form a well that you can draw upon. You gain and use deep beauty and inner wealth as you practice determination, actions, and discipline around your food choices.

Remember this: Nobody can put food into your body except you. This is all about self-care. Nobody else has the control. Only you. So here are six important rules to live and eat by.

RULE 1: YOUR GUT KNOWS BEST

Good health starts in the gut. Yes, your gut is the CEO of your entire body. Your gut gets pissed off when you don't feed it the proper nutrients; eat foods that you are allergic to or can't tolerate well; and unknowingly or knowingly feed it foods that are laced with pesticides, nitrites, sulfides, preservatives, hormones, and dyes. It reacts by bloating, weight gain, constipation, nausea, fatigue, diseases, and much more. Your gut will inevitably make your life miserable.

So prior to meal planning, you've got to know the correct foods to nourish and feed *your* body specifically. Check the labels. Eliminate foods laced with preservatives, GMOs, and other harmful chemicals. Be aware of how your body reacts to certain foods. You can definitely have allergy tests to see about food sensitivity, but in my experience, your gut will often tell you. If you don't feel great after eating, figure it out.

RULE 2: AVOID PROCESSED FOOD

The physical challenges I went through regarding my digestive system are supported by the research of many researchers, including Dr. Amy Lee, a certified internal medicine, nutrition, and obesity medicine specialist who understands the dietary hurdles we all have to overcome.

Dr. Lee believes we are eating a harmful cocktail of preservatives, artificial sweeteners, and other unnatural substances. The difficulty is that it is almost impossible to know what we are putting in our bodies, so you need to be as vigilant as possible. One strategy she suggests is keeping eating out at a minimum. Shopping for and preparing your own meals gives you way more control.

With her focus on education about the hidden problems with food, she is intent on helping people lose weight and get healthy. One thing she focuses on is looking closer at what we think of as healthy food. For example, here are three harmful processed food examples she spotlights; they have high amounts of the fructose corn syrup that she recommends eliminating from your diet:

1. Many supermarket yogurts have twice as much sugar as some cereals. Any yogurt of six ounces should have only thirteen grams of naturally occurring sugar.
2. While wheat bread can be better for you than white bread, store-bought whole wheat breads often contain sizable amounts of high fructose corn syrup.
3. Many supermarket cereal bars and cereals are branded as healthy food options. In truth they are not healthy, because they contain sizable amounts of high fructose corn syrup.[1]

Additionally, food preservatives can cause people serious problems, especially when fast food is a mainstay of your diet. For example, a college student ate only McDonald's for ten days to determine its effects on gut health. The fast food diet left his gut microbes devastated. About 40 percent of his bacteria species were lost, which amounted to about 1,400 different types. Losses of microbial diversity such as this have been linked to diabetes and obesity.[2]

Too many food preservatives can also cause what is called "bad gut bacteria," which results in gas, bloating, heartburn/acid reflux, diarrhea, constipation, irritable bowel syndrome, and other bowel diseases, including Crohn's and ulcerative colitis.[3]

Preservatives have also been linked to overeating and a slower metabolism. Researchers have found that preservatives interfere with our hormones, disrupting the process that tells us when we're full.[4] Additionally, processed food requires less energy from your body to digest because it is high in refined ingredients.[5]

RULE 3: EAT TO AVOID OBESITY

One of the most challenging threats to living a life of inner worth and deep beauty is obesity. It has reached an epidemic in our society and threatens each of us and our loved ones because of its enormous health consequences.

The Institute for Health Metrics and Evaluation (IHME) is an independent global health research organization that provides rigorous and comparable measurement of the world's most important health problems and evaluates the strategies used to address them. Here are some of their findings on obesity:

> An estimated 160 million Americans are either obese or overweight. Nearly three-quarters of American men and more than 60% of women are obese or overweight. These are also major challenges for America's children—nearly 30% of boys and girls under age 20 are either obese or overweight, up from 19% in 1980.
>
> Health risks such as cardiovascular disease, cancer, diabetes, osteoarthritis, and chronic kidney disease increase when a person's BMI exceeds 23. In 2010, obesity and overweight were estimated to have caused 3.4 million deaths globally, most of which were from cardiovascular causes. Research indicates that if left unaddressed, the rise in obesity could lead to future declines in life expectancy in countries worldwide.[6]

Having a food plan and eating to your blood type are vital ways to combat obesity. I also believe that there are natural fat loss supplements that can help you, and there is research to support this belief. Again, please consult with your healthcare professional or dietitian for all nutritional support supplements discussed here.

Taking probiotics is a habit that can really benefit the digestive system, which is intricately connected to our overall health.[7] Lipases, one of our most vital digestive enzymes, is released mainly by the pancreas into the small intestine to help the body process and absorb fats.[8] Every time you eat starchy foods such as potatoes and bread, amylase plays an essential role in breaking those complex carbohydrates into simple, usable sugars.[9] As a protease enzyme, the primary benefit bromelain has is improving protein absorption.[10]

RULE 4: AVOID FOODS THAT HURT YOUR HEART

Heart disease is the leading cause of death in the United States among both men and women. Almost all health professionals recommend gravitating to fruits, vegetables, whole grains, and lean protein if you want to prevent heart disease.

Here is a list of what one health and nutrition expert considers the thirty worst foods for your heart. You may be surprised to find some of these items on the list, but they were selected because of high amounts of salt, fat, and sugars. Please note that some can be modified to make them heart healthy. Pizza is one: There are store-bought variations that are not too bad if you carefully look at the labels.

1. Bacon
2. Beef jerky
3. Biscuits
4. Blended coffees
5. Bouillon cubes
6. Canned vegetables
7. Capers
8. Cheese
9. Chinese take-out
10. Cinnamon rolls
11. Coffee creamer
12. Cold cuts
13. Cottage cheese
14. Diet soda
15. French fries
16. Fried chicken
17. Frozen meals
18. Frozen pies
19. Fruit juice
20. Ice cream
21. Ketchup
22. Margarine
23. Pizza
24. Potato chips
25. Restaurant soup
26. Sausages
27. Steak

28. Tomato sauce
29. Vegetable juice
30. White rice[11]

RULE 5: EAT A VARIED DIET

Variation in your diet is important for two primary reasons. First, it helps you get the essential nutrients you need. Second, it keeps you from getting bored and making bad choices. We don't just eat for fuel. We eat for enjoyment so varying your diet keeps our taste buds happy.

The trick is to eat from the five main food groups that we all learned as schoolchildren. According to the US Department of Agriculture, which introduced food group guidelines in 1916, the five main food groups are:

1. Fruits: The fruit food group encompasses a wide range of fresh fruits and fruit products, including dried, frozen, and canned fruit.
2. Vegetables: The vegetable food group includes an array of fresh vegetables and vegetable products.
3. Grains: The grain food group comprises two subgroups: whole grains and refined grains. Whole grains and their products, including brown rice, quinoa, oats, muesli, and whole wheat pasta, tend to be significantly higher in fiber and protein than refined grain products, such as crackers, corn flakes, grits, and traditional pasta.
4. Protein Foods: Meat, poultry, fish, seafood, eggs, nuts, seeds, soy products, and beans and peas make up the protein food group.
5. Dairy: The dairy food group mostly comprises dairy products that are high in calcium.

RULE 6: SELECT FOODS THAT HELP
YOU AGE AND FIGHT DISEASE

There has been a fair amount of research about food that can help you age and fight disease better. According to one of Canada's leading nutritionists, Leslie Beck, there are foods that have the potential to slow biological aging by acting in a number of ways. They provide unique antioxidants and nutrients that bolster our immune system; they defend against free radicals; they maintain healthy blood glucose and insulin levels; and they help to keep inflammation at bay. Here are some foods that she suggests:

1. Garlic: Loaded with natural sulphur compounds that help to boost your immune system and may keep your heart healthy.
2. Green tea: Rich source of flavonoids, powerful antioxidants that may help to prevent heart disease and certain cancers.
3. Kale: Good source of vitamins A, C, and K; folate; calcium; and potassium; and is plentiful in phytochemicals that help preserve eyesight.
4. Lentils: Great source of soluble fiber (the type that keeps LDL cholesterol in check) along with slow burning, low-glycemic carbohydrates and folate.
5. Oats: Deliver cholesterol-lowering fiber and unique antioxidants called avenanthramides that protect LDL cholesterol particles from free radicals.
6. Olive oil (extra virgin): Excellent source of heart-healthy monounsaturated fat along with vitamin E and anti-inflammatory phytochemicals.
7. Oranges: Packed with vitamin C, a nutrient that keeps your immune system healthy as you age, as well as limonoids, phytochemicals linked with disease protection.
8. Pomegranates: Seeds deliver polyphenols, antioxidants thought to reduce the risk of heart disease and possibly prostate and lung cancer.
9. Red bell peppers: Good source of vitamin C and beta carotene, two antioxidants linked with protection from heart disease and certain cancers.
10. Red grapes: Contain resveratrol, a phytochemical with anticancer and anti-inflammatory properties.
11. Salmon: One of the best sources of omega-3 fatty acids, anti-inflammatories shown to combat aging in cells by preventing special sequences of DNA (called telomeres) from shortening; telomere shortening is linked with the aging process and poorer health.
12. Soybeans: Nutrient-rich and an excellent source of isoflavones, phytochemicals that may help to reduce the risk of breast and prostate cancer.
13. Spinach: Packed with lutein for eye health and a good source of anticancer compounds including vitamins A and C, beta-carotene, and flavonoids.
14. Sweet potatoes: Rich in beta-carotene, a phytochemical that not only protects from free-radical damage, but is also thought to guard against cancer by stimulating communication between cells.[12]

There are also whole, nutrient-dense, organic foods that serve to ward off not only cancer and heart disease but also colds, flu, allergies, and a host of other ailments that plague us every day. They include a variety of beans, other citrus fruits, turmeric, onions, ginger, walnuts, mints, celery, other peppers, and cinnamon.[13]

CREATING YOUR LIFESTYLE MEAL PLAN

Now you are ready to create your own meal plan. I suggest that you plan out one to two weeks of meals. The plan should factor in your blood type and any food intolerances or allergies. You will want to track protein and carbs to make sure you are getting what your body needs. You also need to understand how many calories your body requires. And remember that water is your best friend; drink at least eight glasses a day.

An average woman needs to eat about 2,000 calories per day to maintain her weight and 1,500 calories to lose one pound per week. An average man needs 2,500 calories to maintain, and 2,000 to lose one pound of weight per week. These numbers vary by age, height, current weight, activity levels, metabolic health, and several other factors. There are numerous free calorie counters online for you to calculate the calories in foods.

The jury is still out in terms of research on how frequently you should eat during the day. Some experts advocate every three hours; others say that eating three meals a day is just fine. As I have repeatedly said throughout this book, the only expert on your body is you. So I recommend that you get closely in touch with how you feel during the day. If you need to eat more frequently to feel good, you should do that. If eating more often is a trigger for snacking habits that you want to break, consider three meals a day.

Now I'd like to share my own food plan with you. Table 9.1 shows what one week of my eating would look like. This plan is designed for me to maintain my weight, work with my type O blood, keep processed foods out of my diet, and keep my energy levels up throughout the day through five small meals. Because I am also involved in body building, I created it with my body-building trainer in order to maximize my results.

I recommend that you work with a nutritionist or trainer to create your own plan. Be clear about your objectives. Are you trying to lose weight? Are you preparing for a competition? Are you trying to address specific health issues such as managing diabetes? You need to know exactly why you are creating a food plan and then seek the advice of an expert.

Table 9.1. My Personal Meal Plan

Meal	Food Item	Amount	Calories	Protein (Grams)	Carbs (Grams)
Meal 1	Egg whites	4	68	16	0
7:00 a.m.	Oatmeal	½ c.	150	5	27
	Blueberries	½ c.	41	1	11
Meal 2	Chicken breast	4 oz.	110	24	0
10:00 a.m.	Brown rice	½ c.	115	2.5	20
	Broccoli	1 c.	66	2	15
Meal 3	Chicken breast	4 oz.	110	24	0
1:00 p.m.	Lettuce	2½ c.	150	2	8
	Beans, cucumber, carrots	½ c.	50	2	42
	Nonfat dressing	2 tbsp.	20	1	4
Meal 4	Tilapia	4 oz.	110	23	0
4:00 p.m.	Sweet potato (Optional Item)	1 medium	110	4	25
	Broccoli	1 c.	66	2	15
Meal 5	Chicken breast	4 oz.	110	23	0
7:00 p.m.	Green beans	8 oz.	20	0	5
Total			1296	131.5	172

IMPLEMENTING YOUR PLAN

You are going to be eating a lot fewer prepared foods. You are going to be eating at home more. You are going to look at labels and shop very differently. This means that it is very likely that you will be initially putting more work into preparing food than you have been used to. Over time, it will become second nature. But remember this one statement: *You have to preplan meals to make this work.*

Preplanning puts you in a powerful position in taking care of yourself. If you get discouraged or stray away from the self-care you are giving your body, come back to this list of benefits for a refresher course:

- You will avoid falling into any booby traps that are always lurking around the corner to hinder your success in achieving optimal results.
- You will know exactly what you are feeding your body.
- You will be able to avoid foods that are packed full of excessive chemicals, hormones, food dyes, and GMOs.

- You will be able to work around your food allergies (e.g., dairy, wheat, soy, etc.).
- You will start eating the right foods that will help ignite your health, strength, prosperity, and wellness.
- You will eat out less, thereby not exposing your body to hidden chemicals or food allergies that, like a poison, can cause a reaction.
- You will always have the groceries you need.
- You will eat less or avoid prepackaged foods.
- You will waste fewer groceries.
- You will have the variety of meals that you enjoy to nourish your body.
- You will have less stress about meal planning.
- You will make fewer trips to the grocery store.
- You will be able to control your monthly budget.
- You will save money.

Here are some important pointers to make food preparation easier.

1. Organize. Make sure your kitchen is clean and organized. Be sure that when you take a close look at your kitchen, everything is put away in its proper place. Regardless of the size of your kitchen, create a special area for food prep.
2. Inventory your food pantry. Take an inventory of all of the foods that are in your cabinets, refrigerator, and freezer. Get rid of all foods you may have in your pantry that you know you can no longer eat. If your meal plan requires you to avoid canned or dry foods, you may want to consider donating your nonperishable, canned, and dry foods to a nonprofit food bank. In addition, remember to throw out all expired, old, or tainted foods that you may have discovered.
3. Create your custom grocery list. Creating a grocery list is one of the simplest yet most overlooked components in food prep. I suggest planning meals for at least weeks in advance. Keep in mind, most people's paydays are twice per month, so preparing your meals for two weeks makes it easier for food budgeting and planning. Using technology to create your grocery list makes it easy. You can do it through Siri or apps on your phone.
4. Select useful food containers. I like glass because it is easy to clean, doesn't hold food smells, is dishwasher-safe, and is usable in freezers, microwaves, and ovens. Also, look for containers that are lightweight, easy to carry, and fit in small spaces.
5. Purchase essential utensils. Portion size is incredibly important. Learn how to use a food scale and measuring cups to recognize the

correct serving size. Purchase good, sharp knives and a cutting board so you can prepare foods easily. A slow cooker is also a great time-saving appliance.

6. Fall in love with seasonings. Keep a good supply of herbs, seasonings, and flavored oils to enhance the flavor of your foods. Prepare healthy food with the taste you enjoy.

7. Select a food prep day. Once you have a clean and organized kitchen with food containers and all of your supplies, you are ready to prep and cook. I normally prep my food for the week on a Sunday, but choose the time that works for you. After your food is ready, organize your food into separate storage food containers and label them.

Now, let's get ready for the next chapter, where you will learn more about your body type. Once you get your meal plan and body type down to a science, you will enjoy all of the remarkable benefits of your journey toward transforming your life through self-care.

HOW OFTEN SHOULD YOU EAT?

There are no rules that are set in stone when it comes to how many meals you should eat per day. However, I'd like to circle back to one fact: Your body is unique and special. So let your body guide you to what is best for your blood and body type, based on your new eating habits, time of day, and how often you are eating.

When I was training to go on stage for competition, I was planning on eating six small, balanced meals per day. If you stop and think about it, would you say that seems like a lot of food? For me it was. No matter how hard I tried, I just seemed to never get to that last meal. Why? It was because my stomach was full. That's my point. Your stomach knows when to stop, and we must learn to listen to our gut because it knows best.

Here's another way to look at how often to eat, specifically when it's highly restrictive eating. When you are driving your car and there is no gas in the tank, your car is going to stop. That is the way your body works. Your metabolism will slow down, and your body will think you're starving it. So your smart body starts storing fat, because your body has no idea when you are going to feed it again. Just stop and think about it. Isn't that counterproductive?

Some research indicates that eating six small meals a day does not offer weight loss benefits.[14] However, in my work with clients, I have observed other benefits of eating small meals every three to four hours.

- You are less likely to make bad choices when you are eating every three to four hours.
- After three hours, blood sugar levels start to decrease. Then you may start feeling a little weak and a little hungry.
- If you have not had a meal in five hours, blood sugar levels are low and you are at a higher risk of making poor food choices. That's when you might start overeating.

LISTEN TO YOUR BODY

Let's take a closer look at what your body is telling you with regard to whether you should eat. You may experience one or more of the following:

- Light-headedness
- A growling stomach
- A headache coming on
- Dropping blood sugar
- Bloated and/or stomach pain

EATING BEST PRACTICES

- Eat small healthy meals and snacks.
- Keep snacks small.
- Let your fist be your guide, as in choosing a fistful of nuts.
- A piece of fruit is a perfect snack.
- Chew your food; eat slowly.
- Stop eating before you feel too full.
- Always listen to what your body's gut (the CEO) is telling you.
- Remember to always eat according to your preplanned meals.
- Avoid the traps of overeating by not allowing yourself to get too hungry.
- Always stay in check and control your portion size.
- Always avoid eating two to three hours before your bedtime.
- Drink a glass of water and/or herbal tea to help you relax.
- Avoid snacks with sugar; the sugar spikes may disrupt your sleep.

"DEVELOPING YOUR OWN MEAL PLAN" QUESTIONS

Open up your binder or computer and answer the following questions to help you on your self-care discipline journey:

1. What is your ultimate goal in creating a lifestyle with healthier food selections?
2. Have you ever developed a meal plan before? If so, what was it? And did you get the results you were expecting? If not, why not?
3. After eating, do you have any challenges with the side effects or symptoms of bloating, weight gain, constipation, nausea, and fatigue? If so, how do you manage them? Have you shared your experience with your doctor and/or dietitian yet? If so, what was their recommendation?
4. Have you checked with a trusted healthcare professional about taking any vitamins, herbs, and/or nutritional supplements yet? If so, what was his or her recommendation?
5. List the foods and beverages you are currently eating on a daily basis.
6. How much water are you drinking on a daily basis? Do you think you need to drink more or less? Or are you on point?
7. Are you eating foods that are laced with preservatives, GMOs, and other harmful chemicals? Create a list of the processed foods you are currently consuming.
8. Are you willing to look for healthier alternative food choices to replace the processed food you are consuming? Create your alternative food list.
9. What actions have you taken to reorganizing your kitchen? List each action and check it off your list as you complete each item, such as cabinets, refrigerator, and freezer.
10. Create a list of essential utensils, containers, bottles, and so forth that you will need for your food prepping and storage.
11. Create your custom grocery list for your new lifestyle meal plans.
12. Create your custom meal plan chart for one week at a time. Use the sample from this chapter and modify it to meet your needs. Remember, the chart is only a guide for you to use to create your custom meal plan.
13. Have you selected a day and time for prepping your food? What is the day of the week you have chosen? And what is your backup food prep day?

14. How are you feeling at this moment? Are you excited about taking ownership of your health by contributing toward transforming your life through self-care? Describe your feelings.
15. Are you committed to giving your new meal plan a try for at least twelve weeks? Create a journal just for your daily meal checklist to keep you focused and on point.

· 10 ·

How to Exercise for Your Body Type and Abilities

*C*ongratulations! You've made it halfway through your wellness lifestyle journey. Now we are going to focus on exercise. Before we delve deep into this area, it is important to understand your body type. People are forever asking me, "Carolyn, how often do you work out?" or "What types of exercises do you focus on?" The answer is that I've learned to *customize* my workouts for my body type and my physical challenges. That's what you will learn to do in this chapter.

Once you know your body type, your trainer can help you develop workouts that will focus on your specific needs. With consistency, you will soon start to lose those unwanted pounds, get in better shape, and experience a more sculptured body. In time, your body will start craving more exercise, and your daily routine will become more comfortable. That's what's in it for you.

You also need to understand any physical challenges that you might have that will require adjustments of exercise routines. Once again, this is a place where working with your health team is critical. This may include your physician, physical therapist, trainer, and others.

But first let's talk about why exercise is so important.

PRESERVING YOUR BODY

Whether you're nine or ninety, abundant evidence shows exercise can enhance your health and well-being. Unfortunately for many people, sedentary pastimes such as watching television, surfing the internet, or playing computer and video games have replaced more active pursuits. Millions of

Americans simply aren't moving enough to meet the minimum threshold for good health—burning at least seven hundred to one thousand calories a week through physical pursuits.

Decades of science confirm that exercise improves health and can extend your life. Adding as little as a half an hour of moderately intense physical activity to your day can help you avoid a host of serious ailments, including heart disease, diabetes, depression, and several types of cancer, particularly breast and colon cancers. Regular exercise can also help you sleep better, reduce stress, control your weight, brighten your mood, sharpen your mental functioning, and improve your sex life.

In a nutshell, exercise does the following:

- Reduces your chances of getting heart disease. For those who already have heart disease, exercise reduces the chances of dying from it.
- Lowers your risk of developing hypertension and diabetes.
- Reduces your risk for colon cancer and some other forms of cancer.
- Improves your mood and mental functioning.
- Keeps your bones strong and joints healthy.
- Helps you maintain a healthy weight.
- Helps you maintain your independence well into your later years.[1]

Given those benefits, who wouldn't incorporate exercise as a vital part of their self-care program? It's time to use the discipline, determination, and actions we have talked about so far in this book to make exercising an integral part of your daily life. You are worth it. Remember your deep beauty and inner worth.

COMPONENTS OF AN EXERCISE PROGRAM

A well-rounded exercise program has four components: cardio activity, strength training, flexibility training, and balance exercises. Each benefits your body in a different way.

- Cardio: Cardio or aerobic exercise is the centerpiece of any fitness program. Nearly all of the research regarding the disease-fighting benefits of exercise revolves around cardiovascular activity, which includes walking, jogging, swimming, and cycling. Experts recommend working out at moderate intensity when you perform aerobic exercise. Brisk walking that quickens your breathing is one example.

- Strength training: Strength or resistance training, such as elastic-band workouts and the use of weight machines or free weights, is important for building muscle and protecting bone.
- Flexibility training: Stretching is the third prong of a balanced exercise program. Muscles tend to shorten and weaken with age. Shorter, stiffer muscle fibers make you vulnerable to injuries, back pain, and stress. But regularly performing exercises that isolate and stretch the elastic fibers surrounding your muscles and tendons can counteract this process.
- Balance exercises: Balance erodes over time, so balance exercises are one of the best ways to protect against falls. Balance exercises take only a few minutes and often fit easily into the warm-up portion of a workout. Many strength-training exercises also serve as balance exercises, and you can add them into other forms of exercise, such as tai chi, yoga, and Pilates.[2]

When you start exercising, you may feel some pain or soreness. In addition to stretching, try icing the area for twenty minutes several times a day for the first two to three days after the pain begins. Or use heat on the area after the first few days.

The types of exercises you do within each of these four categories should be right for your body type if you want to maximize your workouts and get the shape you desire. Let me share with you how I accidentally learned—the hard way—about my own body type when I was in my late thirties.

MY OWN EXPERIENCE WITH BODY TYPES

I had been working out tirelessly on my own for months with the aim of shedding a few pounds. I remember just how hard it was for me. No matter how hard I was working out, I never lost a pound, and I never got the fitness results I was looking forward to achieving.

Then, I realized I needed a personal trainer so I interviewed one from the local gym. Before making a decision on hiring him, I shared my very clear vision of what I wanted my body to look like. "I want to have a firm, sculptured, and tight body. But I do not want to get overly muscular because my body tends to bulk up easily. Can you help me reach my goals?"

He assured me it would not be a problem. Guess what? A few weeks later, I looked like the Incredible Ms. Hulk. My trainer did not know how to train or recommend figure-enhancing exercises for me. In fact, in a very short time, my body bulked up so much that I could not fit into my clothes. Yes, he got me into great shape, but it was not the body shape I was expecting or found pleasing.

This compelled me to look deeper into what happened to my body and why. The first thing I learned was a few relevant facts about the three different body types: ectomorph, mesomorph, and endomorph. I discovered that my body type was a mesomorph, which is a naturally athletic body type. That was one of the reasons why my body bulked up so fast. The exercises were not tailored to me specifically.

Based on my experience, I also discovered that all personal trainers might not have the knowledge or expertise to provide a healthy workout regimen for your unique body type. I cannot express how imperative it is for you to thoroughly vet the fitness specialist whom you have chosen before making your final decision. Hiring a personal fitness trainer can be a costly investment toward your future health and wellness lifestyle but well worth it to get you on track.

Remember, if you are considering hiring a personal trainer, it is a best practice for you to learn all you can about your body type first. Know that fitness should never be a "one size fits all." Always be sure to hire only certified training professionals with expertise in body-matching exercises and the knowledge to help you work around any physical injuries and disabilities that you may have as well.

IDENTIFYING YOUR BODY TYPE

Let's begin with three simple and short definitions of the body types mentioned above. You may have some qualities of each in your body, but most people have one primary type.

- Ectomorph: Lean and long, with difficulty building muscle.
- Mesomorph: Muscular and well-built and highly suited to muscle-building activities like body building.
- Endomorph: Large, often pear-shaped, with a lot of body fat and a high tendency to store it.[3]

Now let's dive a little deeper into the descriptions to help you assess your own body. Ectomorphs have narrower frames, thinner bones, and smaller joints, and they may be flatter in the chest and butt. A distance runner, fashion model, or ballerina would probably have this body type. Ectomorphs often process food quickly and find it hard to put on weight.

Mesomorphs generally have large muscles and a large bone structure. If you want to get into body building, this is the best body type to have. For mesomorphs, gaining and losing weight is easy.[4]

Endomorphs are often pear-shaped with a high tendency to store body fat. They often have more body fat and muscle, smaller shoulders, shorter limbs, and a larger bone structure like football linemen, shot put throwers, or curvier women. They often gain weight easily and especially in their belly and hips, partially because they store high-carb foods as fat instead of burning them.[5]

Now take a look at figure 10.1 and go look in a mirror. Where do you see yourself? What is your primary type? If you are unclear, ask someone to give you his or her assessment. Remember, there is not a *right* body type. This is just the body type you have been given. What you do with it is up to you.

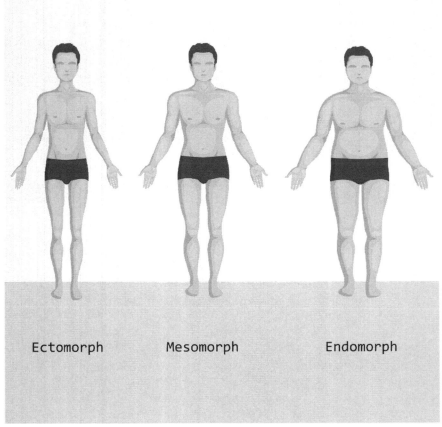

Figure 10.1.   Man body types, from fat to fitness. Eveleen007 dreamstime.com

Fitness Planning for Ectomorphs

Research shows that ectomorphs may look skinny and find it hard to put on weight, but they can have more body fat than you think, especially as they age.[6] They have the ability to develop lean muscle quickly and easily. Ectomorphs need to be careful not to overtrain.

If you are an ectomorph, here is general advice to help you design your fitness workout, followed by an example of a day-by-day training program in table 10.1.

1. Exercise one hour per day, Monday through Friday. Treat Saturday and Sunday as optional days to work out.
2. Warm up with five minutes of stretching and five minutes of aerobics.
3. Complete at least three sets of each exercise, and rest thirty to ninety seconds after each set.
4. Train each muscle group once per week at a very low-medium repetition.
5. Select free weights that are heavy enough that you can only complete six to ten reps. This is the ideal range for putting on size.
6. Keep workouts short and very intense. High Intensity Interval Training (HIIT) workouts are great.
7. Stretch for five to fifteen minutes after your weight lifting workout.
8. Keep cardio to a minimum to avoid weight loss.
9. Balance exercises can help you prevent and avoid falls; practice balancing exercises for five to ten minutes.
10. Do cardio two times per week at a training heart rate of x beats per minute (bpm; over age 50, 120 bpm; under age 50, 150 bpm). Do one five-minute cardio warm-up, ten minutes at your training heart rate, and a ten-minute cool-down/stretch.
11. If you are doing body building, focus only on a few big free-weight compound exercises, like squats, bench, and deadlift.

Table 10.1. Sample Exercise Plan for Ectomorph

Ectomorph	Cardio[1]	Strength	Flexibility	Balance
Monday		**Warm-up:** 5-minute stretching, 10-minute cardio. Make sure the weight is heavy enough that you can only complete 5 repetitions. **Chest and Back:** Push and pull exercises. Perform 8 to 10 sets repetitions, for 4 separate times. **Abs:** Crushes is a modified set-up for back safety. 3–15 sets repetitions, 3 separate times.	5- to 15-minute stretching: • Knees to chest exercise • Cobra or modified cobra exercise • Seated hip stretch exercise • Standing hamstring stretch exercise • Seated spinal twist exercise • Knee to shoulder exercise	5 to 10 minutes of • Tai chi and balance • One-legged balance • Leg swings Make sure you have assistance if you need it.
Tuesday	5-minute cardio warm-up, 10 minutes at your training heart rate, and 10-minute cool down/stretch.	**Abs:** Crushes is a modified set-up for back safety. 3–15 sets repetitions, 3 separate times.	Post-workout, 5 to 15 minutes stretching: • Knees to chest exercise • Cobra or modified cobra exercise • Seated hip stretch exercise • Standing hamstring stretch exercise • Seated spinal twist exercise • Knee to shoulder exercise	5 to 10 minutes of • Tai chi and balance • One-legged balance • Leg swings Make sure you have assistance if you need it.
Wednesday		**Warm-up:** 10-minute stretching, 5-minute cardio. Make sure the weight is heavy enough that you can only complete 5 repetitions. Focus *only* on a few big free weights or compound exercises (squat, bench, deadlift, etc.). **Legs and Hips:** Push and pull exercises. Perform 6 to 12 repetitions, for 4 separate times. **Abs:** Crushes is a modified set-up for back safety. 3–15 sets repetitions, 3 separate times.	Cooldown: Post-workout, 5 to 15 minutes stretching: • Knees to chest exercise • Cobra or modified cobra exercise • Seated hip stretch exercise • Standing hamstring stretch exercise • Seated spinal twist exercise • Knee to shoulder exercise	5 to 10 minutes of • Tai chi and balance • One-legged Balance • Leg swings Make sure you have assistance if you need it.

Ectomorph	Cardio[1]	Strength	Flexibility	Balance
Thursday	Treadmill, swimming, water aerobics, walking, seated bicycle, dancing, low-moderate impact aerobics for 20 minutes maximum.	**Abs:** Crushes is a modified set-up for back safety. 3–15 sets repetitions, 3 separate times.	**Cooldown:** Post-workout, 5 to 15 minutes stretching: • Knees to chest exercise • Cobra or modified cobra exercise • Seated hip stretch exercise • Standing hamstring stretch exercise • Seated spinal twist exercise • Knee to shoulder exercise	5 to 15 minutes of • Tai chi and balance • One-legged balance • Leg swings Make sure you have assistance if you need it.
Friday		**Warm-up:** 5-minute stretching, 10-minute cardio. Make sure the weight is heavy enough that you can only complete 5 repetitions. **Arms and Shoulders:** Push and pull exercise. Focus *only* on 4–5 repetitions maximum. **Abs:** Crushes is a modified set-up for back safety. 3–15 sets repetitions, 3 separate times.		
Saturday/ Sunday	Meditate for at least 5–10 minutes or longer every day. Select a time that is best for you.	Rest.		

1. Note: You do not want to overtrain for this body type. Consult with your fitness trainer. Modify to your specific health needs.

Fitness Planning for Mesomorphs

Mesomorphs have naturally athletic bodies, large bone structure, and dense muscle mass. They have an ideal body type for body building. If you are a mesomorph, here is general advice to design your fitness workout, followed by a sample plan in table 10.2.

1. Exercise one hour per day Monday through Friday. Treat Saturday and Sunday as optional days to work out.
2. Warm up with five minutes of stretching and five minutes of aerobics.
3. Do cardio three to five times per week at a training heart rate of x beats per minute (bpm; over age 50, 120 bpm; under age 50, 150 bpm). Do one five-minute cardio warm-up, ten minutes at your training heart rate, and a ten-minute cool-down/stretch.
4. Lift medium to heaver weights—with minimal rest in between each set. Complete at least three sets of each exercise, and rest thirty to ninety seconds after each set.
5. Train three days per week.
6. Perform eight to twelve reps of three to four exercises for each muscle group.
7. Allow plenty of warm-up and cool-down time to protect the ankles, knees, and hips.
8. If body building, five days a week of weight training is ideal to stimulate muscle growth.
9. If preparing for a competition, do cardio twice a day.

Table 10.2.   Sample Exercise Plan for Mesomorph

Mesomorph	Cardio	Strength	Flexibility	Balance
Monday	Five-minute cardio warm-up, 10 minutes training at your heart rate, and 10-minute cool-down/ stretch. Modify to your specific health needs.	Warm-up. 5–15 minute stretching Use: Light, medium or heavy weights— depending on what your fitness goals are. Consult with your fitness trainer. **Chest and Back** Push and pull exercises. **Perform** 8 to 15 sets repetitions, for 4 separate times. **Abs:** Crushes is a modified set-up for back safety. 15 sets repetitions, 3 separate times.	Post-workout 5–15 minute stretching. • Knees to chest exercise • Cobra or modified cobra exercise • Seated hip stretch exercise • Standing hamstring stretch exercise • Seated spinal twist exercise • Knee to shoulder exercise	Improve Balance, Avoid Falls. (Optional) 5–15 minutes. • Tai chi and balance • One-legged balance • Leg swings Make sure you have assistance if you need it.
Tuesday	Five-minute cardio warm-up, 10 minutes training at your heart rate, and 10-minute cool-down/ stretch	**Abs:** Crushes is a modified set-up for back safety. 3–15 sets repetitions, 3 separate times.	Post-workout 5–15 minute stretching. • Knees to chest exercise • Cobra or modified cobra exercise • Seated hip stretch exercise • Standing hamstring stretch exercise • Seated spinal twist exercise • Knee to shoulder exercise	Improve Balance, Avoid Falls. (Optional) 5–15 minutes. • Tai chi and balance • One-legged balance • Leg swings Make sure you have assistance if you need it.
Wednesday	Five-minute cardio warm-up, 10 minutes training at your heart rate, and 10-minute cool-down/ stretch.	Warm-up. 5–15 minute stretching **Arms and Shoulders** Push and pull exercise. **Perform** 8 to 15 sets repetitions, for 4 separate times. Use: Light, medium or heavy weights. Or advised by your fitness trainer. **Abs:** Crushes is a modified set-up for back safety. 15 sets repetitions, 3 separate times.	Post-workout 5–15 minute stretching. • Knees to chest exercise • Cobra or modified cobra exercise • Seated hip stretch exercise • Standing hamstring stretch exercise • Seated spinal twist exercise • Knee to shoulder exercise	Improve Balance, Avoid Falls. (Optional) 5–15 minutes. • Tai chi and balance • One-legged balance • Leg swings Make sure you have assistance if you need it.

(continued)

Table 10.2. *(continued)*

Mesomorph	Cardio	Strength	Flexibility	Balance
Thursday	Treadmill, swimming, water aerobics, walking, seated bicycle, dancing, low–moderate impact aerobics. Aim for 60 minutes maximum.	**Abs:** Crushes is a modified set-up for back safety. 3–15 sets repetitions, 3 separate times.	Post-workout 5–15 minute stretching. • Knees to chest exercise • Cobra or modified cobra exercise • Seated hip stretch exercise • Standing hamstring stretch exercise • Seated spinal twist exercise • Knee to shoulder exercise	Improve Balance, Avoid Falls. 5–15 minutes. (Optional) • Tai chi and balance • One-legged balance • Leg swings Make sure you have assistance if you need it.
Friday	Five-minute cardio warm-up, 10 minutes training at your heart rate, and 10-minute cool-down/ stretch.	Warm-up. 5–15 minute stretching **Legs and Hips** Push and pull exercise. **Perform** 6 to 12 repetitions, for 4 separate times. Use: Light, medium or heavy weights. Or compound exercises (squat, bench, deadlift, etc.) Or advised by your fitness trainer. **Abs:** Crushes is a modified set-up for back safety. 15 sets repetitions, 3 separate times.	Post-workout 5–15 minute stretching. • Knees to chest exercise • Cobra or modified cobra exercise • Seated hip stretch exercise • Standing hamstring stretch exercise • Seated spinal twist exercise • Knee to shoulder exercise	Improve Balance, Avoid Falls. (Optional) 5–15 minutes. • Tai chi and balance • One-legged balance • Leg swings Make sure you have assistance if you need it.
Saturday/ Sunday	Meditate for at least 5–10 minutes or longer everyday. Select a time that is best for you.	Rest		

Fitness Planning for Endomorphs

Endomorphs usually have a more significant amount of body fat and muscle. They have the capacity for high fat accumulation and storage. In addition, endomorphs are known to have smaller shoulders, shorter legs and arms with a larger bone structure. If you are an endomorph, here is general advice to design your fitness workout, followed by a sample plan in table 10.3.

1. Exercise one hour per day, Monday through Friday. Treat Saturday and Sunday as optional days to work out.
2. Warm up with five minutes of stretching and ten minutes of cardio.
3. Do cardio five times per week for five to ten minutes to start, and then a five-minute cool-down/stretch. Increase your time as you get stronger. *Optimal Cardio goal:* Do one five-minute cardio warm-up, ten minutes at your training heart rate, and a ten-minute cool-down/stretch. The training heart rate is expressed in beats per minute (bpm; over age 50, 120 bpm; under age 50, 150 bpm).
4. Allow plenty of warm-up and cool-down time to protect the ankles, knees, and hips.
5. Do strength training three days per week.
6. To avoid plateaus, change the exercise mix often. Add new exercises and subtract old ones. Frequently change the exercise order, as well.
7. Focus on lifting routines that build endurance rather than size.
8. Lift weights light enough that you can complete at least 15 repetitions per set and take relatively short rest breaks between sets.
9. Include both compound and isolation movements in weight training.
10. Avoid training too heavy, too often.
11. Stretch for five to fifteen minutes after your weight lifting workout.

Table 10.3. Sample Exercise Plan for Endomorphs

Endomorph	Cardio	Strength	Flexibility	Balance
Monday	5 to 10 minutes to start; 5-minute cool-down/stretch. *Or* Optimal cardio goal: 5-minute warm-up, 10 minutes at your training heart rate, and 10-minute cool-down/stretch. Increase your time as you get stronger. Modify to your specific health needs.	**Warm-up:** 5-minute stretching. Use light weights. Aim to complete 15 repetitions or as advised by your fitness trainer. **Chest and Back:** Push and pull exercises. Perform 8 to 12 sets repetitions, for 4 separate times. **Abs:** Crushes is a modified set-up for back safety. 3–5 sets repetitions, for 3 separate times.	**Cool down:** Post-workout, 5- to 15-minute stretching: • Knees to chest exercise • Cobra or modified cobra exercise • Seated hip stretch exercise • Standing hamstring stretch exercise • Seated spinal twist exercise • Knee to shoulder exercise	5 to 15 minutes of • Tai chi and balance • One-legged balance • Leg swings Make sure you have assistance if you need it.
Tuesday	5 to 10 minutes to start; 5-minute cool-down/stretch. *Or* Optimal cardio goal: 5-minute warm-up, 10 minutes at your training heart rate, and 10-minute cool-down/stretch. Increase your time as you get stronger. Modify to your specific health needs.	**Warm-up.** 5-minute stretching. Use light to medium weights or compound exercises (squat, bench, deadlift, etc.) or as advised by your fitness trainer. **Legs and Hips:** Push and pull exercise. Perform 6 to 12 repetitions, for 4 separate times. **Abs:** Crushes is a modified set-up for back safety. 3–5 sets repetitions, for 3 separate times.	**Cool down:** Post-workout, 5- to 15-minute stretching: • Knees to chest exercise • Cobra or modified cobra exercise • Seated hip stretch exercise • Standing hamstring stretch exercise • Seated spinal twist exercise • Knee to shoulder exercise	5 to 15 minutes of • Tai chi and balance • One-legged balance • Leg swings Make sure you have assistance if you need it.
Wednesday	5 to 10 minutes to start; 5-minute cool-down/stretch. *Or* Optimal cardio goal: 5-minute warm-up, 10 minutes at your training heart rate, and 10-minute cool-down/stretch. Increase your time as you get stronger. Modify to your specific health needs.	Use light to medium weights or as advised by your fitness trainer. **Arms and Shoulders:** Push and pull exercise. Perform 8 to 12 sets repetitions, for 4 separate times. **Abs:** Crushes is a modified set-up for back safety. 3–5 sets repetitions, for 3 separate times.	**Cool down:** Post-workout, 5 to 15 minutes stretching: • Knees to chest exercise • Cobra or modified cobra exercise • Seated hip stretch exercise • Standing hamstring stretch exercise • Seated spinal twist exercise • Knee to shoulder exercise	5 to 15 minutes of • Tai chi and balance • One-legged balance • Leg swings Make sure you have assistance if you need it.

Endomorph	Cardio	Strength	Flexibility	Balance
Thursday	5 to 10 minutes to start; 5-minute cool-down/stretch. Treadmill, swimming, water aerobics, walking, seated bicycle, low-impact aerobics, dancing. Aim for 45 minutes.	Modify if needed. **Abs:** Crushes is a modified set-up for back safety. 3–15 sets repetitions, 3 separate times.	**Cool down:** Post-workout, 5 to 15 minutes stretching: • Knees to chest exercise • Cobra or modified cobra exercise • Seated hip stretch exercise • Standing hamstring stretch exercise • Seated spinal twist exercise • Knee to shoulder exercise	5 to 15 minutes of • Tai chi and balance • One-legged balance • Leg swings Make sure you have assistance if you need it.
Friday	5 to 10 minutes to start; 5-minute cool-down/stretch. *Or* Optimal cardio goal: 5-minute warm-up, 10 minutes at your training heart rate, and 10-minute cool-down/ stretch. Increase your time as you get stronger. Modify to your specific health needs.	Use light to medium weights or compound exercises (squat, bench, deadlift, etc.) or as advised by your fitness trainer. **Legs and Hips:** Push and pull exercise. Perform 6 to 12 repetitions, for 4 separate times. **Abs:** Crushes is a modified set-up for back safety. 3–5 sets repetitions, for 3 separate times.	**Cool down:** Post-workout, 5 to 15 minutes stretching: • Knees to chest exercise • Cobra or modified cobra exercise • Seated hip stretch exercise • Standing hamstring stretch exercise • Seated spinal twist exercise • Knee to shoulder exercise	5 to 15 minutes of • Tai chi and balance • One-legged balance • Leg swings Make sure you have assistance if you need it.
Saturday/ Sunday	Meditate for at least 5–10 minutes or longer every day. Select a time that is best for you.	Rest.		

DON'T LET PHYSICAL LIMITATIONS STOP YOU

Have you thought about what exercises you can do if you have limited body movement or physical challenges? Many of us have some limitations because of age, accidents, or diseases. That should not stop you from exercising.

You just need to know your body very well, understand your physical limitations, and work with your healthcare professionals to design the right plan for you. I like to think of it as using your *different abilities* to the best of your ability.

One of my friends and inspiration is Jose Flores. At forty-one, he is a husband, father of two sons, and the author of *Don't Let Your Struggle Become Your Standard!* As a toddler, he was diagnosed with spinal muscular atrophy (SMA), a neuromuscular disease that weakens the muscles. Today he is in a wheelchair.

Growing up wasn't easy for Jose. He suffered from many insecurities and feelings of insignificance, not knowing where he would end up in life. One day he made a choice to start living life to the fullest and not caring about what other people thought about him. Through his perseverance and faith in God, he has been able to overcome many obstacles.

I asked him about his exercise routine. He said, "Carolyn, I love getting into the swimming pool and doing my water exercises, because when I am in the pool my body is free. In the pool, I can do strength training fitness and squats, which is a compound full body exercise that strengthens my primary muscles, such as the thighs, hips, and buttocks all at the same time. Also, I can sit on the lower steps in the pool, and push my legs out and pull them back repeatedly. I feel so great after a good water aerobics. I try to get to the pool at least once a week."

He had an alternative for the days he could not get to the pool: "I work out in my wheelchair. It has an apparatus that helps me with muscle contractions and generates a functional movement that will lift my legs and lower my head, allowing me to repeat this action as many times as I want to keep my muscles moving. It is a great workout for my heart."

Then he said some words that will always serve as a great inspiration to me: "Carolyn, my disability is visible; the world can see my limitations. But other people may have secret limitations—limitations in one's mind, the fear of failure, negative thinking, poor performance, lack of self-worth, complacency, and the list can go on and on."

FITNESS PLANNING FOR DIFFERENT ABILITIES

Be sure to incorporate exercises that are developed by physical therapists and trainers who understand your abilities. Daily exercises will help improve flexibility, stability, and muscle and bone strength. Make sure that you have assistance in exercises when you need it, and understand your abilities to stand or lie on the floor. Here are some general guidelines in developing your fitness program:

1. Aim high: Never allow your limitations to stop you. Be sure only to work with professionals with specific expertise in training and working "around" your injuries and/or restrictions. This is an absolute must to prevent any additional injuries.
2. Be sure to take an active role in planning and the development of your weekly fitness schedule. Always feel free to ask questions and or share any concerns you may have with your trainer. Remember, your trainer is your fitness partner—when you achieve a milestone, he or she does, too.
3. When you are training, remember to always take your time with each set of exercises. Take each set of your activities nice and slow. Aim for quality only, during each exercise routine.
4. Embrace your custom-built exercise plan, created just for you. Keep in mind that this is not a race. Be sure to start out slow and keep building as you go. Each week you can add or adjust your exercise plan as needed.
5. Ignite the fire and deep beauty within you every day. Make no excuses.
6. Evaluate and review your progress biweekly.

SPECIFIC EXERCISES AND ADVICE FOR DIFFERENT ABILITIES

Stretches may provide some relief for people experiencing pain related to sciatica (backache). However, people with backache should speak to a doctor before doing any sciatica stretches, to avoid further injury. A doctor or physical therapist may recommend that people perform several of the following stretches each day.

Seated Hip Stretch

1. Sit in a chair with your feet on the floor and knees bent at a ninety-degree angle.
2. Raise the affected leg up and cross that ankle over the opposite knee.
3. Gently bend forward over the crossed leg, breathing deeply and holding for 15 to 30 seconds before releasing. Do the same with the opposite leg. Repeat.

Standing Hamstring Stretch

1. Start by standing tall with feet together.
2. Lift the affected leg straight out in front of you and rest the heel on a ledge or table that is just slightly higher than your hip.
3. Keeping the knee straight but soft, bend forward at the waist, keeping the spine straight until you feel a stretch in the back of the leg.
4. Hold the stretch for fifteen to thirty seconds before releasing.
5. Return to the starting position then repeat on the other side.

Additional Stretches

• Knees to chest
• Cobra or modified cobra
• Seated spinal twist
• Knee to shoulder[7]

Frozen shoulder is a condition in which the shoulder is stiff, painful, and has limited motion in all directions. Stretching exercises are usually the cornerstone of treating frozen shoulder.

Cross-Body Reach

Sit or stand. Use your good arm to lift your affected arm at the elbow, and bring it up and across your body, exerting gentle pressure to stretch the shoulder. Hold the stretch for fifteen to twenty seconds. Do this ten to twenty times per day.

Towel Stretch

1. Hold one end of a three-foot-long towel behind your back and grab the opposite end with your other hand.
2. Hold the towel in a horizontal position.

3. Use your good arm to pull the affected arm upward to stretch it.
4. You can also do an advanced version of this exercise with the towel draped over your good shoulder. Hold the bottom of the towel with the affected arm and pull it toward the lower back with the unaffected arm. Do this ten to twenty times a day.[8]

IMPROVING BALANCE

Falls are one of the primary causes of death and life-changing injuries. Improving your balance is particularly important as you age and generally important to all people who are practicing self-care. Here are some ways to improve your balance:

- Tai chi helps improve balance because it targets all the physical components needed to stay upright—leg strength, flexibility, range of motion, and reflexes—all of which tend to decline with age.[9]
- One-legged stands are the quintessential balance exercise. Stand behind a sturdy chair, grasping the chair lightly for support.
  - One-legged balance is a great beginner's move. Keep a stable chair or a wall within an arm's reach. With feet together, pick up one foot with the knee facing forward or to the side. Hold the position with eyes open, then closed. Switch feet and repeat for four reps on each foot.
  - Leg swings: Stand on your right leg and raise the left leg three to six inches off the floor. With arms at your sides, swing your left leg forward and backward, touching the floor for balance, while keeping your torso erect. Now, repeat the moves, but don't allow your foot to touch the ground. And finally, swing the left foot to the left side, holding the right arm out. Switch legs and repeat.
  - One-legged clock with arms: Balance on one leg, with the torso straight, head up, and hands on the hips. Visualize a clock and point your arm straight overhead to twelve, then to the side at three, and then circle low and around to nine without losing your balance. Increase the challenge by having a partner call out the different times to you. Switch to the opposite arm and leg and repeat.
  - Single-leg dead lift: Balance on your left foot, engage the abs, and bend forward at the hips while reaching toward the ground with your right hand. Hold on to a five- to ten-pound weight, and raise your right leg behind you for counterbalance. Tighten the buttocks as you return to the starting position. Keep your knee relaxed and your back flat throughout the movement. Switch legs.[10]

YOUR CUSTOMIZED WORKOUT PLAN

Now we are going to do something a little different. I want you to pull out your binder or computer. It is crucial that you know *all* the details of your body from head to toe in order to design a customized workout plan. Let's walk through these steps. Remember, you need to contact your trusted healthcare professionals to tell them about your new plan and get their input.

Step 1

1. Do you know your body mass index (BMI)? If so, what is it? If not please request that your trusted healthcare professional, certified trainer, or dietitian check your BMI.
2. What's your attitude? Do you know that your attitude is everything when you start a new healthy lifestyle change? Now, on a scale of one to ten, what is your current attitude? If your attitude is on the lower end, what action do you think will help you to raise your attitude to a higher level? Explain.

Step 2

1. Which body type are you? Ectomorph, mesomorph, or endomorph? How do you know? Explain.
2. In your personal journal, create a twelve-week custom body chart to track your progress. You can duplicate the sample in table 10.4.
3. Start out by tracking your weight biweekly so you will not get discouraged. Once you get your groove on—are on track and fully committed—then you can adjust your tracking system as you go.
4. Nutrition has a major influence on our overall body response and success. Consult with your dietitian or other trusted healthcare professional for tips on what supplements are best for you.

Table 10.4. Custom Body Chart Example

Age	Height	Weight	Neck size	Bust size	Waist size
Shoulder size	Arms size	Wrist size	Hip size	Thigh size	Calve size
Ankle size	Shirt	Pants size	Dress size		

Step 3

1. Wear lightweight and loose fabrics; you do not want to feel restricted while you are training. Well-designed activewear should feel like a second skin.
2. Wear breathable attire made of sweat-resisting fabrics that will draw moisture away from the body, leaving you feeling dry and comfortable.
3. Wear high-quality athletic shoes with flexible soles, appropriate thread for their function, and the ability to absorb impact.
4. Purchase proper headgear, earphones, earplugs, stopwatches, tennis rackets, water aerobic gear, and water bottles.
5. Look your best because that way you will actually feel better about your workout, especially when you are looking in the mirror as you exercise. The systematic influence that clothes have on the wearer's psychological processes is called "enclothed cognition."

"HOW TO EXERCISE FOR YOUR BODY TYPE AND ABILITIES" QUESTIONS

Keep your binder or computer open, and answer the following:

1. What body type do you have: ectomorph, mesomorph, or endomorph? How did you discover it?
2. What type of results are you looking to achieve by matching your body type to exercise?
3. What type of cardio exercises do you enjoy the most? Why?
4. What do you like about strength training? How do you know if you are doing it correctly?
5. How would you rate your level of flexibility? What can you do to improve it?
6. How would you rate your balance? What can you do to improve it?
7. Do you have any physical injuries, and or disabilities? If so, do you have a trusted healthcare professional whom you can consult with in moving forward to an exercise plan?

Dealing with Stress

In the last chapter, we discussed how to develop an exercise plan and how exercise can significantly reduce stress, tension, and anxiety when you go and have a good sweaty workout. Now we are going to focus more specifically on other strategies to combat stress, which is a threat to you living the life you want and deserve.

I strongly believe taking ownership of the stresses you are dealing with will give you the power to make transformations in every area of your life. But the fact is that we all respond to stress in very different ways. Stress is natural. It is our bodies' defense against danger, and it flushes our bodies with hormones to prepare for or confront danger. You've heard it described as the "fight or flight" response.

The symptoms of stress are both physical and psychological. But here's the catch: While short-term stress is helpful in preparing to face danger, long-term stress is dangerous to our health. That's why learning ways to manage stress are really important.[1]

I'd like to share my personal story about how I deal with stress as well as train you on a healthier different way to think and respond to stress. Because I encountered so many stress events in my life, I became an accidental expert on how to deal with stress. I have had many hands-on experiences in dealing with unbelievable stress that might have crushed many people.

Throughout this book, I've shared my life's journey, addressing my physical life-changing injuries, family woes, betrayal in my marriage, crushed career, and financial challenges. While I was dealing with the facts of life, it left me with only two choices: either sink or swim.

One thing I know for sure: It took me a while to learn how not to focus on the problems that were causing me to feel stressed or anxious. Over time,

I've learned to shift my thinking and search for solutions. Once I started focusing on resolving my problems, then my stressful situations appeared to become more manageable for me to resolve.

Case in point: Have you ever had a personal invitation to have a meeting with an IRS agent? Isn't that what you would consider one of the scariest things on earth? Because I had never had this type of experience before, my first reaction was one of panic. However, at the same time I wondered, why am I panicking? I've done nothing wrong; this must be a mistake.

The time came to meet the IRS agent, and I must say, it turned out to be a great learning experience for me. Why do I say that? It's because I learned directly a few significant tax tips as well as the careless mistakes that my tax person of ten years had made. Also, I learned that my tax person of ten years had been sourcing out my taxes.

What was my lesson learned? I discontinued services with my tax person, and now I have only trusted tax consultants with appropriate credentials and a proven track record. Getting an invitation for an audit is an experience you never want to have. Luckily for me, I had all of my financial records for the requested three-year review. Thank God.

Now let's examine eight lessons that I have learned that you can apply to your own life.

LESSON 1: TRANSFORM YOUR THINKING

The first thing I want to share with you is that I still deal with some form of stress. Notice that I said "deal with." Yes, how you choose to deal with and manage your stress is entirely up to you.

I am a strong believer in choosing one's battles. Have you thought about why you're stressing and what's truly causing your stress? During many interviews, people have shared with me that often they feel stressed and they don't know why. I believe once you find out what's really causing your stress, then you will be able to address the issue, problem, or concern. This will transform the way you think about and resolve your situation.

We all experience some type of adversity because it's just a part of life. Whether you are dealing with family matters, health concerns, financial setbacks, career or workplace challenges, you can't let the stresses drag you down. But in order to do that, you have to name the stress clearly. You have to know the why and what. Otherwise, it becomes scarier and unmanageable. You need to acknowledge, face, and own the facts of what's causing your stresses. If you are in denial of what's causing your stress, it will be virtually impossible to change your situation.

LESSON 2: DON'T NORMALIZE STRESS

Often, people get so caught up in having stress in their lives that they develop a mindset of just waiting for the next shoe to drop. When happy times come, they are not living in the present moment to embrace it.

Have you ever heard a person say, "This experience is too good to be true" or "I'd better enjoy it while I can because I know something is going to happen" or "Good things don't last forever"? I believe that people who think like that have developed a habit of accepting stress as normal. So they live a life filled with stress, never recognizing or appreciating the good times and great moments when they come.

LESSON 3: CREATE A MINDSET FOR CHANGE

Train your mind to think differently, just as we discussed in previous chapters. When you are feeling stress, train your mind to think something great and tell yourself you will not tolerate stress.

In my case, I changed the way I looked at my stresses by helping others transform their lives through self-care and deal with the stress of caring for a loved one. Once I created this vision, I had to study and learn the specifics of how to help others. Words can't express the joy I received from helping others in my family, community, and in the world. My healing came from helping others, which allowed me to deal with my stresses head-on.

That was a healthy outcome of not just focusing on myself. Life is far too short to live a life of stress and anxieties.

LESSON 4: PLAN FOR SUDDEN
AND UNEXPECTED STRESSES

Unfortunately, unexpected life emergencies happen all the time. What do you do when you have a sudden and unexpected life emergency? It's a best practice to have a plan in place way before you are in a situation that could throw you off guard and cause you unnecessary stresses that can paralyze your efforts. This allows you to stop what you are doing, stay calm, and activate your plan.

Here is a short list of questions that make up the foundation of an emergency plan that will help you reduce stress:

1. Do you have an emergency checklist of people to call if you or someone you love is in an accident?
2. Do you have a trusted person who knows your passwords, doctor information, and other key fundamentals in your life just in case you are incapacitated?
3. Do you know the above for members of your family?
4. Do you have a proper ID that can be easily recognized?
5. Have you clearly identified any medical issues or medicines that you need? Do you have that information for everyone in your family?
6. Do you have an escape plan in case of a natural emergency, like a hurricane, or unnatural emergency, like a fire?
7. Have you communicated the plan to members of your family?
8. Have you made provisions for any animals that live with you?
9. Do you have a supply of food and water in case of an emergency?
10. Do you have a mentor, partner, or friend to call to assist you when you need help?

These are just examples of planning for the unexpected emergency that will help guide you in stressful situations. Don't allow the unexpected stress to cause you to crumble. When you have a plan in place, you will be able to survive and thrive in spite of the added tension.

LESSON 5: SELECT HEALTHY COPING SKILLS

Many people turn to unhealthy behaviors to cope with or escape their stress, such as drinking too much alcohol, self-medicating on drugs, and overeating. But when you change the way you look at your stresses and anxieties, you will be able to manage your discomfort with stress more positively and productively.

Face your stresses and choose healthy activities, like going for a walk, exercising, painting, journaling your thoughts, reading, practicing your faith, and meditating. Create your own wellness by training your mind to think differently by practicing your favorite hobby.

LESSON 6: KEEP YOUR LIFE BALANCED

Often, to avoid facing difficulties, people overload their calendars with social activities. Others deal with stress by withdrawing from family and friends. The best practice is to strike a balance by maintaining a healthy social life even when you're stressed. But also schedule the time to be alone with your thoughts by creating "me time."

LESSON 7: ACKNOWLEDGE YOUR CHOICES

People often feel like victims when they experience circumstances that seem out of their control. Always remember, from the time you wake up until the time you go to sleep, you have the power deep within your soul to choose how you will respond to any stressful situation. Sometimes you have to have the courage to just say no to things you don't want to do, and you must be willing to accept the responsibilities for the choices you have made. Acknowledging and taking ownership of the decisions you have made is your key to greater happiness and freedom.

LESSON 8: DISCOVER YOUR RAINBOW

When you control your emotions, you won't see the world through rose-colored glasses, the blue of depression, or the red of anger. Instead, you can pragmatically acknowledge that there often is a silver lining in each circumstance—that good things can come from stressful situations. Instead of letting your hardship turn you into a resentful, angry, or helpless victim, you will choose and use your stressful situations as your guiding light to becoming a stronger and a healthier-thinking person.

FIFTEEN THINGS YOU CAN DO TODAY

Here's my summary list of fifteen things you can do today to reduce stress in your life.

1. Ban the habit of accepting stress as normal.
2. Face your problems head-on.
3. Plan for the unexpected.
4. Stand up for what you believe.
5. Decide to live your life in a beautiful state of being.
6. Go for a walk, exercise, paint, or meditate.
7. Believe that you can train your mind to think differently.
8. Keep and view your problems in the proper perspective.

9. Find something you want to serve that is greater than yourself.
10. Know that you can handle difficulties when they arrive.
11. Surround yourself with positive and like-minded people.
12. Raise your standards in all areas of your life.
13. Understand that stress can actually drive you to do greater things in your life.
14. Practice your spiritual beliefs every day.
15. Go and give someone a great big hug. You will be amazed at how good it will make you and the other person feel.

"DEALING WITH STRESS" QUESTIONS

Now it's your time to pull out your binder or computer to answer these questions to help you formulate a plan on how to deal with stress in a healthy and helpful manner.

1. Do you know why you are experiencing stress? If so, write your why.
2. Are you in denial of the stresses in your life? Why haven't you faced your stresses head-on? What's stopping you?
3. Do you take ownership of your stress? How so? And if you are not taking ownership of your stresses, why?
4. How have you turned your stresses into learning and growth opportunities? List them.
5. What are your coping skills when you are dealing with stress? List them.
6. How do you react when you are dealing with sudden and unexpected stressful situations? Do you have a plan in place for the just-in-case emergencies? What's your plan?
7. How do you keep your life balanced when you are dealing with stress?
8. List situations in your life in which you've turned the stress around, resulting in positive changes.
9. Have you made the decision to live your life in a beautiful state of being? How are you doing it?
10. How are you managing your stress through fitness? Create a list.
11. Have you thought about taking the focus off yourself and volunteering your time to help someone else who is in need? Do you see how volunteering can become a great benefit in helping you manage your stress? If so, how?

· 12 ·

Incorporating Meditation into Self-Care

*I*n the last chapter, we talked about stress and healthy ways of managing, responding to, and dealing with stress. One of the strategies I recommended was practicing daily meditation. Now it's time to explore the why, what, and how of this powerful way to manage stress and dramatically change your life. Let's start with the place that often gives us the most insight: the why.

WHY IS MEDITATION IMPORTANT?

Just think about it. When was the last time you stopped just for a moment to breathe or take a time-out to care of yourself mentally, emotionally, and spiritually by just doing nothing except being quiet and living in the moment?

In today's fast-paced world, it is so easy to get caught up with your long to-do list and family, health, financial, career, and other pressing obligations. And technology keeps us connected 24/7, to the extent that we don't even unplug when on vacation or sleeping.

Because of this, we frequently forget to stop and reflect on our own mental and spiritual well-being. As a nation, we have become far too busy or technology-obsessed to take the time to recognize the importance of nourishing, rebuilding, and connecting our mind, body, and spirit.

Researchers continue to examine how meditation can help treat high blood pressure, irritable bowel syndrome, pain, and psychological disorders. Like the blood type diet and body typing exercises, more research is needed into the area of meditation. However, people who use this technique throughout the world report an improved attitude toward life and reduction of issues like stress, anxiety, and depression. Meditation also is being used to help people quit smoking as well as other addictive behaviors.[1]

WHAT IS MEDITATION?

Meditation is a mind and body practice that focuses on the interaction between the brain, mind, body, and behavior. There is some evidence that meditation actually changes different areas of the brain. As Alice G. Walton, a health writer for *Forbes* with a PhD in biopsychology and behavioral neuroscience, explains:

> There's been a lot of discussion about what kinds of mental activities are actually capable of changing the brain. Some promises of bolstered IQ and enhanced brain function via specially-designed "brain games" have fizzled out. Meanwhile, meditation and mindfulness training have accumulated some impressive evidence, suggesting that the practices can change not only the structure and function of the brain but also our behavior and moment-to-moment experience.[2]

The experts from Mindworks, who are accomplished meditators, scholars, psychologists, and professionals, describe meditation best:

> Meditation is simply a method of calming the mind and achieving self-awareness using an assortment of techniques for working with the mind. Although a lot of things in life might be beyond human control, it's quite possible to have much more control over our minds: what we think, feel and perceive about ourselves and others as well.[3]

In addition, Mindworks interviewed accomplished meditation expert, Trinlay Rinpoche. She says,

> Our happiness doesn't stem from external factors or material pursuits. Rather, the main source of our happiness comes from within us. Using meditation, we can tune our minds to access the wealth of happiness that already exists within us. And when we access our most basic qualities, we show kindness, compassion and other expressions of goodness to others.[4]

Meditation has been known since the early nineteenth century and has been practiced in various religious traditions and beliefs worldwide. In the United States, the number of adults who meditated in 2012 was estimated at eighteen million.[5] I suspect the number is substantially higher today, as our interest in alternative ways of healing our bodies and minds increases.

The following are different types of meditations. You are likely to find one that is just right for you. The most commonly taught form of meditation is mindfulness meditation.

- Buddhist meditation means seated "Zen" or "meditation," in Japanese.
- Guided meditation is a modern phenomenon and an easy way to start meditating.
- Spiritual meditation is the mindful practice of connection to something that is greater, richer, and deeper than oneself.
- Mindfulness meditation is an adaptation of traditional Buddhist meditation practices.
- Yoga meditations include several meditation types taught in the yoga tradition.
- Christian meditation is usually practiced with the purpose of transcending the mind and attaining enlightenment.
- Loving kindness meditation derives from a Pali word (*Metta* meditation) that means kindness, benevolence, and goodwill.
- Mantra meditation (OM meditation) uses a mantra: a syllable or word that is repeated for the purpose of focusing your mind.
- Transcendental meditation (TM) is a specific form of mantra meditation.
- Self-enquiry/"I Am" meditation stresses investigating our true nature to find the answer to "Who am I?"
- Vipassana meditation is a traditional Buddhist practice that has been adapted to modern times.
- Taoist meditations focus on the generation, transformation, and circulation of inner energy by quieting the body and mind, unifying body and spirit, finding inner peace, and harmonizing with the Tao.
- Qigong (Chi kung) is a Chinese word that means "life energy cultivation" and is a body-mind exercise for health, meditation, and martial arts training.
- Sufi meditation is based on Sufism, where the goal is to purify oneself and achieve mystical union with the Supreme (named Allah in this tradition).[6]

MY PERSONAL MEDITATION JOURNEY

For many years, I tried practicing mindful meditation. I wanted so badly to experience the wellness benefits of what I'd heard about meditation. But, for some reason, I was never able to focus during my meditation sessions. I could not control or calm my mind from drifting everywhere. I just could not stop my mind from thinking. I even wondered if I was trying too hard to meditate and prevent my mind from wandering back to my to-do list. I just didn't know how to let go, relax, and be free until I met Beatriz Osorno.

Beatriz is known for her guided meditations through the sounds of vibration, which is a guided healing meditation that brings awareness to each of the seven chakras, or energy centers, in the body. She incorporates the violet flame—to transmute the light of love, healing, and forgiveness—to heal the body, mind, and soul.

Chakras, which date back to India thousands of years ago, are used during meditation to focus attention and cleanse the body. The seven chakras are:

1. The Root Chakra is located at the base of the spine and helps us maintain a sense of being on a firm and solid ground with inner stability.
2. The Sacral Chakra is located at the pelvis and helps us regulate our emotions and desires and not to be driven by them.
3. The Navel Chakra is located at the navel center and helps us digest not only our food but also our life experiences.
4. The Heart Chakra is located at the heart center and helps us tap into unconditional love. Its energetic function is to help us find authentic self-expression.
5. The Throat Chakra is located near the base of the throat and also helps us find authentic self-expression.
6. The Third-Eye Chakra is located between the eyebrows and helps us learn to know ourselves emotionally, mentally, and spiritually.
7. The Crown Chakra is located at the crown of the head and helps us function in a more enlightened way, cultivate self-mastery, and find a sense of connection with all.[7]

The way I met Beatriz was not merely by chance. Three different people on different occasions during discussions about meditation mentioned her name. So one day, I decided to attend one of her sessions. At that point, I did not have a clue about chakras.

I had a profound experience I will never forget. For the first time, my mind did not drift; I felt the sensation of internal peace, happiness, and love. Finally, I experienced the nourishing and spiritual effects of meditation that I had been seeking for years. I was ready to spiritually grow through the sounds of vibration and violet flame meditation techniques of healing the body, mind, and soul.

HOW TO GET STARTED

I was persistent about meditation and finally found a method that worked for me. You don't need to go through the journey guideless, as I was for such a long time. Instead, here are seven easy steps you can take to begin meditating now:

1. Choose a consistent time so you can develop the habit of meditating daily.
2. Find a quiet and comfortable space. Minimize light exposure. I highly suggest starting out in the sitting position to learn.
3. Be sure that you are hydrated and have gone to the bathroom.
4. Practice your breathing. Notice how you feel when the air is moving through your nostrils and pay close attention between inhaling and exhaling.
5. Incorporate free guided meditations online to help get you started. Sites like the Chopra Center have great ones.
6. Schedule at least two to three minutes a day when you first start. Then slowly add additional time.
7. Discover which type of meditation is best for you, and master it.

MEDITATION, DEPRESSION, AND WEIGHT LOSS

One of the people who told me about meditation was my dear friend Anthony. His story was so compelling to me because whenever I'd run into Anthony at our local gym, he always had a peaceful presence. I told him how I admired his calmness. He said, "I don't want you to think that my life has always been like this."

He explained that he was forty-two years old and, when he got his first job out of high school, he thought he was going to work for the company for the rest of his life. He loved his job and worked his way up to a management position. "I thought I had it made, and I was living the American dream," he said. Then one day after 19 years of services his management position was dissolved and he was handed a severance package. For the first time in his life, he found himself unemployed. And he could not find work anywhere. After ten weeks of being unemployed, he became depressed. Then something came over him.

"I knew I had to start meditating again to help calm my spirit and to stop my downward spiral of feeling depressed. I made the commitment and started meditating like I used to do before my life got so busy that somehow I had forgotten about how meditation used to help me. Once I started attending guided meditation sessions again, I just felt more relaxed. I began to recognize that maybe losing my job was a benefit to my health. I had somehow gained twenty-five pounds, and I never thought about how the extra weight was affecting my health."

Shortly afterward, he was recruited for a job with a Fortune 500 company. "Boy, was I excited. This time, however, before I went on this interview, I did something I have never done before. I sat in my car and meditated for twenty minutes before my roundtable interview with four people. I was very relaxed, confident, and sincere all within myself. After the meeting was over, I felt that I had nailed it."

Less than twenty-four hours later, the recruiter contacted him with a job offer with a substantial increase in salary and benefits. And after he started his new job, he lost the twenty-five pounds.

MEDITATION AND FOOD

One of the major reasons why people eat is stress. It therefore makes sense that since meditation relieves stress, it can be useful in helping put you back on the road to healthy eating.

One idea I like especially is to use meditation to reduce food cravings. Fr. Jamie Zimmerman suggests learning how to handle food cravings with awareness and intention:

> You'll use the acronym STOP to help you through moments of fear and weakness. "S" stands for simply that: stop. "T" stands for "take three deep breaths." "O" stands for "observe." "P" stands for "proceed," in a way that supports you and those around you. You'll use this acronym to understand where the craving is coming from and what it means. What thoughts are going through your head right now? What is your craving telling you? What do you imagine will happen if you act on the craving? Breathe deeply and allow yourself to discover what you truly need.[8]

"INCORPORATING MEDITATION INTO SELF-CARE" QUESTIONS

Open up your binder or computer, and answer the following questions.

1. What is your past experience regarding meditation? Write your experience.

2. Are you currently practicing meditation? If so, what type of meditation, and what is the benefit of meditation for you?
3. When you meditate, are you clearly focused or does your mind have a tendency to start drifting? How do you think you can get focus?
4. How is meditation benefiting you? Make a list of benefits.
5. If you have never practiced meditation before, when do you plan to get started?
6. Are you ready to go to the next level of meditation? If so, what do you plan to practice?

· 13 ·

The Real Connection
between Health and Money

*H*erophilus, the ancient Greek physician said, "When health is absent, wealth is useless." Another sage, the Roman poet Virgil, said it in a different way: "The greatest wealth is health." Both of these wise men recognized that riches do not mean a thing if you do not have your health.

The opposite is also true, however. If you don't have money, it is harder to have health. Having money makes it easier to be healthier much of the time. You have money for trainers, health clubs, trips to relax, supplements, and, of course, medical care.

Unfortunately, substantial evidence also exists that poverty is linked to poor health. Stress on individuals and families; lack of access to medical, dental, and vision care; long working hours; and reliance on cheaper but often less nutritious foods increase health risks and make children especially vulnerable.

One area in which money and health are very closely connected is the issue of obesity. A 2011 George Washington University study concluded the average annual cost of being obese was $4,879 for women and $2,646 for men, based on indirect costs such as diminished productivity and direct costs such as medical care. An obese woman could have almost $600,000 in savings and an obese man more than $320,000 if the added costs were invested at five percent annual return over a forty-year career.[1]

So as you see, how you relate to health and money are connected. If you don't have your health, what good is your money—except to pay for the high cost of healthcare? If you have good health, you can take care of yourself and create a life of gratefulness, happiness, and joy. Remember, the secret to enjoying your life is to stay healthy in mind, body, and spirit.

The person who taught me about the connection between health and money was not one of the ancient sages but my father. As he said, "Never trade your health for the appearance of wealth. Always live within your means, and stay out of debt."

In the 1960s, my dad was an astute businessman, entrepreneur, and an avid runner. As a preteen, I can recall many times I'd joined him as he ran around the lake in Denver, Colorado. Being so young and not really understanding the health benefits of running, one day I asked him, "Why do you like running around the lake?" His reply was, "You've got to keep your body moving so sickness can't catch up with you."

He also taught me at an early age about the principles of money management and how to respect money. Looking back, I can clearly see that my dad was showing and telling me how health and money clearly go hand in hand. What is the lesson here? Teach your kids early about the real facts and the connection between health and money.

This lesson served me well later in life. Earlier in this book, I shared my personal story about making a high six-figure income and then experiencing several unexpected life-changing incidents that put my health and finances in a dramatic downward spiral that I had never expected. This led to a panic attack so severe that I thought I was having a heart attack.

That experience opened my eyes to not be afraid to face my health afflictions and dwindling finances. Instead, I fought for my health, finances, peace of mind, and well-being. I faced my unexpected health and financial affairs head on. Once I met and embraced my fears, I immediately began to delve entirely into total self-care, which included my relationship with health and money. I started studying everything I could get my hands on about handling my health and finances. I took back the authority over my life, got my butt up, and ended the pity party.

When it comes to your health and finances, take a stand when you fall. Get right back up, create a new you, and rebuild your health and wealth through your God-given talents. No, I'm not a CPA, attorney, or a physician. But I am a person who has experienced life's ups and downs and twists and turns. Through it all, I made up my mind to never ever give up.

THE ROLE OF DISCIPLINE

Throughout this book, I have talked about the importance of discipline in self-care—to take control of your health, reduce stress, eat well, and exercise routinely. It also plays a role in how you spend and make money.

Researchers have found that demonstrating self-control in one area of a person's life affects other areas. So if you exercise discipline in money matters, you can apply that discipline to health. And if you build up discipline in your eating habits and fitness routines, you can gain the discipline you need to manage your money better as well.[2]

Sounds reasonable, right? Below is some excellent advice from Luvleen Sidhu, cofounder, president, and chief strategy officer at Bank Mobile. At age twenty-nine, the Harvard University and Wharton Business School graduate truly gets the connection between health and money matters. Four aspects are shown here.

Keep Your Mind Sharp

"Success is not a matter of chance or luck; it's based on hard work, dedication, and the ability to execute the right decisions at the right times. Whether you work a corporate job or are an entrepreneur, many of the business decisions you make will require that you have a sharp analytical mind. Feeding your body the right nutrients is vital in providing your brain with the nourishment it needs to function at its full capacity. Conversely, feeding your body the wrong things can make you sluggish and slow down your ability to make the right decisions needed to succeed, survive, and thrive in business."[3]

Exercise Your Body for Increased Energy

"For the most part, building wealth and maintaining a level of success takes more than working 40 hours a week. At the end of it all, you may be feeling fatigue and want to take a power nap to recoup just to find yourself even more tired than when you began. Well, according to WebMD, a walk or light jog may be better than a nap for boosting energy and fighting fatigue. Other studies have also shown that morning workouts are best because they help your body produce more adrenaline at the beginning of the day, which helps you power through your routine to give you more energy throughout the day."[4]

Staying Healthy Keeps You Out of the Hospital

"I may be stating the obvious, but there is no way you can build wealth and increase your net worth if you're sick. The foods you decide to eat and the amount of exercise you do will have a direct effect on your health. Eating right and exercising will not only keep you out of the hospital, but it will also keep you away from needing to take medications that usually have many side effects, possibly including fatigue (among other things that are counter to what you need to be on top of your game)."[5]

Never Give Up

"As stated earlier, maintaining good habits in one area may trickle down to other areas in your life. It's no secret that on your journey to greatness many obstacles may try to stop you from achieving your goals. However, you must keep going when the going gets tough. This level of perseverance can be taught and trained."[6]

PLANNING FOR EMERGENCIES

Financial problems can lead to health problems and vice versa—a cycle that can become a costly catch-22. Financial stress can cause anxiety, migraines, insomnia, and other physical ailments. It also can mean skipping routine medical checkups, not discovering essential issues about your health, and making poor dietary and other lifestyle choices. Over time, this can lead to more significant, costlier health problems, which in turn can produce ever-greater financial distress.[7]

At its extreme, medical incidents can drive people to financial ruin. Over 60 percent of all bankruptcies in the United States in 2007 were driven by medical incidents. The share of bankruptcies attributable to medical problems rose by 50 percent between 2001 and 2007.[8]

I firmly believe that one of the most critical parts of your financial and health planning is to have insurance. Countless individuals do not take the necessary precautions to insure themselves for sudden and unexpected emergencies. As a direct result, out-of-pocket expenses can be devastating and overwhelming.

You probably will need several different types of insurance policies if you want to safeguard your health and finances to live a comfortable economic existence. In my case, a close friend, Thell Dodd, a former financial analyst, mentored me. Thell, who is twenty years older than I am, talked in detail about the importance of having insurance and the different types of insurance policies to consider, such as homeowners, auto, disability, health, life, and long-term care policies. I remember her saying, "Carolyn, you are only in your thirties and you're healthy. This is the time you need to get prepared for the just-in-case." Years later, I can't tell you how grateful I am that I listened to my friend.

GETTING RID OF DEBT

My finances have ranged from earning a high income to having no income. I have experienced large debt such as student loans, mortgage, and the high cost of medical expenses. I have also experienced paying off all of my debt, too. Too often, once you're debt-free, a sudden and unexpected emergency may show its ugly face, causing you to go into debt again. But today I strongly believe your goal is to always live a debt-free life. It is an amazing feeling to live a life that is free and clear of debt.

Nearly fifteen years ago I had the opportunity to learn from the financial guru Dave Ramsey. Boy, did my life change drastically once I understood his concepts on finances and started implementing his economic principles. It was the first time I had ever experienced a debt-free life.

I've learned that when you stick to his concepts, it becomes easy to save money and even have money to invest. Getting out of debt happens quickly once you learn how to apply this concept to your life. Budgeting is made more manageable, and the money-related aspects of your marriage and other relationships can become smoother.

Here is what Ramsey describes as the seven baby steps to living debt-free:

1. Save $1,000 to start an emergency fund.
2. Pay off all debt using the debt snowball method. (I will explain this in a second.)
3. Save three to six months of expenses for emergencies.
4. Invest 15 percent of your household income into Roth IRAs and pretax retirement funds.
5. Save for your children's college fund.
6. Pay off your home early.
7. Build wealth, and give.[9]

What is the debt snowball method? You start out by getting organized and disciplined with your finances by following the four steps shown here.

Step 1: Write Down Your Total Income

This is your total take-home (after taxes) pay for both you and, if you're married, your spouse. Don't forget to include everything—full-time jobs, second jobs, freelance pay, Social Security checks, and any other ongoing source of income.

Step 2: List Your Expenses

Think about your regular bills (mortgage, electricity, etc.) and your irregular bills (quarterly payments like insurance or HOA) that are due for the upcoming month and prorate. After that, total your other costs, like groceries, gas, subscriptions, entertainment, and clothing. Every dollar you spend should be accounted for.

Step 3: Subtract Expenses from Income to Equal Zero[10]

This is zero-based or "EveryDollar" budgeting, meaning your income minus your expenses should equal zero. When you do that, you know that every dollar you make has a place in your budget. If you're over or under, check your math or simply return to the previous step and try again.

Step 4: Track Your Spending

Once you create your budget, track your spending. It's the only way you will know if your spending is aligned with your plan. EveryDollar makes tracking your expenses (and budgeting for them) extremely easy. Visit EveryDollar .com to learn more.[11]

HERE'S HOW THE DEBT SNOWBALL WORKS

Step 1: List your debts from smallest to largest.

Step 2: Make minimum payments on all debts except the smallest— throw as much money as you can at that one. Once that debt is gone, take its payment and apply it to the next smallest debt while continuing to make minimum payments on the rest.

Step 3: Repeat this method as you plow your way through debt. The more you pay off, the more your freed-up money grows—like a snowball rolling downhill.[12]

THINGS TO CONSIDER

Have you thought about cutting back your spending and paying off all your debt? Have you considered downsizing your home? Do you need to do some spring cleaning and get rid of the stuff that no longer serves any purpose? Can you imagine spending less time on the exhausting treadmill of life and, instead, living life the way it was meant to be?

Then I suggest that you start out by connecting with your health and financial matters by taking action today. Yes, you do have a say in your life. Remember, "No excuses. Find a way. Believe for a miracle. Press on till you win. *Don't quit!*"

"THE REAL CONNECTION BETWEEN HEALTH AND MONEY" QUESTIONS

Now, it's your time to pull out your binder or computer to think about and answer these questions:

1. What is your relationship with your health and money? Explain.
2. What is your level of discipline over your health, and finances? Are you more disciplined over one than the other? What action(s) can you take to create a balance?
3. Do you have a trusted financial adviser, CPA, and/or attorney who can guide you with money matters? If so, who is he or she? If not, have you considered speaking to one?
4. Do you have insurance policies in place for sudden and unexpected emergencies? If so, what are they? If not, when will you start?
5. Are you ready to get out of debt? If so, when do you plan to take action?
6. When do you plan to start saving for your future? Create your action plan.

• *14* •

Living Your Purpose

So far I have focused on self-care through diet, exercise, improved relationships, stress reduction, meditation, and even finances. I have talked about defining moments and discipline as well as how to be the authority of your life.

Most importantly, you have seen that tapping into your deep beauty is a circular process. You need to practice self-care to achieve deep beauty and inner worth, and you need to draw on the well of deep beauty and inner worth to transform your life through self-care.

The concept I would like to discuss now is how to live your purpose. You may ask, "Don't you need to have a purpose before you can begin embracing self-care?" I don't think so.

Yes, it would be nice. In my experience, however, it is really difficult to have a clear purpose if your life is in turmoil. As you start transforming your life, often purpose becomes clearer and your need to live it every day increases in importance. You no longer want to simply survive. You find yourself with a deep desire to thrive.

For those reasons, I decided not to start this book talking about purpose. Instead, I first wanted you to become grounded in the ideas and actions around self-care. Quite simply, you need to start practicing self-care to find your purpose and transform your life. But now you may be ready to focus on purpose—specifically, your divine purpose.

FINDING YOUR DIVINE PURPOSE

One of the most inspirational books I have ever read is *The Top Five Regrets of the Dying: A Life Transformed by the Dearly Departing*, in which Bronnie

Ware eloquently writes about her personal journey and how she followed her calling.

After years of unfulfilling work, she found herself working in palliative care. There she tended to the needs of those who were dying and in doing so transformed her own life. She wrote a blog that was read by more than three million people in its first year about the most common regrets expressed to her by the people she had cared for.

By applying the lessons of those nearing their death to her own life, she developed an understanding that it is possible for people to die with peace of mind—if they make the right choices. Here are the top five regrets she learned from the people she cared for as they were dying. They have heavily influenced my own thoughts on living a life of purpose.

1. I wish I'd had the courage to live a life true to myself, not the life others expected of me.
2. I wish I didn't work so hard.
3. I wish I'd had the courage to express my feelings.
4. I wish I had stayed in touch with my friends.
5. I wish that I had let myself be happier.[1]

I believe the best way to live a life without regrets and transform your life through self-care is to embrace your divine purpose. What is great about living your divine purpose is that your cultural background, age, sex, race, religion, or language does not matter.

Everyone is born with a special gift and a divine purpose to make a difference in life. Within that purpose is a unique talent just waiting to be explored and expressed. Divine purpose is big. Just stop for a moment, and think about the last time you witnessed someone fulfilling his or her life's purpose.

Picture yourself watching your favorite female athlete win multiple Olympic medals. Imagine that she has stated that her purpose in life—her divine purpose—is to become the best in the world at a specific sport. Along the way, she gets there by winning national competitions, overcoming an injury, and beating her own personal best time. And after winning the Olympics, she goes even deeper and realizes her divine purpose is to inspire young girls to be their best. She becomes a motivational speaker and starts a nonprofit, all to fulfill that divine purpose of inspiring young women.

You have met people like this throughout your life. Maybe their stories are not so dramatic, but they have deep meaning. Maybe it is a man who starts a company that focuses on technology to produce food in healthier ways. Maybe it is a husband and wife who take in foster children. Maybe it is a young man who joins the Peace Corps and brings new cottage businesses to impoverished communities.

All have a sense of their divine purpose. The common denominator is that their divine purpose drives them to cultivate and master their unique gifts. It's incredibly inspiring to observe them as they radiate happiness and joy.

One of my favorite quotes about divine purpose is by Maria Shriver: "It's always inspiring to me to meet people who feel that they can make a difference in the world. That's their motive, that's their passion. . . . I think that's what makes your life meaningful, that's what fills your own heart and that's what gives you purpose."[2]

To find your divine purpose, you need to be living *in your own divine light.* Are you living in your divine light or are you living your life based on someone else's opinion about you? I used to be that way. I was a people-pleaser because I did not want to hurt anyone's feelings. I ignored my own feelings because I wanted to fit in. At that time, I had no idea that I was not living in my divine purpose. I only knew that I did not want to rock the boat.

Frequently life's circumstances will try to dictate how you should live your life versus living your life in divine calling, light, purpose, and peace. When you are living in the divine light with purpose, you will recognize those life-defining moments that change your life forever.

Always remember, you were born with a special gift and a divine purpose to make a difference in the world. Start walking in your divine light with your purpose and mission. Embrace the divine light within you, which you are destined to live. And know that the divine light belongs to and in you because *you* are the divine light.

To quote Dr. Wayne Dyer, a man who has inspired millions, "With everything that has happened to you, you can either feel sorry for yourself or treat what has happened as a gift. Everything is either an opportunity to grow or an obstacle to keep you from growing. You get to choose."[3]

WHERE ACTIONS FIT IN

Of course, there is a significant difference between *having* a purpose and *living* a purpose. Many people can describe their purpose, but when you examine their actions, you'll find a disconnect.

I have one client who said his whole purpose was to make his family happy. When he came to work with me, he was eighty pounds overweight with high blood pressure; he was spending twelve hours a day at his highly stressful job. At forty-eight, he was a heart attack waiting to happen. But he really thought he was making his family happy because he was providing them with an upscale lifestyle.

With three children under twelve, how was he going to make his family happy and provide for them if he became sick or even died? What if his non-stop work led to issues in his marriage and ended in divorce? And, perhaps most importantly, what about the thing he was unconsciously withholding from his family: a loving and nondistracted father and husband?

We worked together to help him find balance in his life. He reevaluated the parts of his relationship with his children and wife—he was acting like their caregiver all of the time—so they took more responsibility. He took a look at his job and made a very healthy switch to a different company. He changed his diet to his blood type and developed an exercise plan to his body type. He even took up meditation.

Now healthy and content with himself, his home life, and work, he is really living his purpose to make his family happy by being an amazing husband and father. He is doing it by practicing self-care and tapping into his deep beauty and inner worth.

I have another client, a woman in her late thirties, whose great passion is travel. Her purpose was to tour the world and write about her adventures. However, she was convinced she would never be able to do it.

Because of a car accident in her teens, she had ongoing pain in her back in addition to anxiety when she was in an automobile. After consulting with her health team, she began working with me. I helped her become the authority in her life. She had an aha moment when she understood that if she could manage her pain and develop plans to work around her anxiety with cars, then she would be able to achieve her purpose.

Through various diet, exercise, and supplement changes, which were all approved by her doctor, she began managing her pain. Then we built out a realistic travel plan that would allow her to travel to Europe at a pace that honored her body and relied on public transportation to minimize time in cars. We worked on meditation techniques to help her manage stress and anxiety when she needed to take automobiles.

She learned that the key to achieving her purpose was to practice self-care. I cannot tell you what it meant to me when I got postcards from Paris, London, and Zurich, all with one single line: "Living my purpose! Thank you!"

I could tell you story after story. And I suspect you would see yourself in many of them. The trick is to find your purpose and live it.

Often people ask me, how do you know your divine purpose? The simplest way for me to describe it is as a feeling in your heart and soul that you just can't let go of. Many times, I've tried to walk away from my divine purpose, but it keeps drawing me back. Remember the words from my radio guest, fifteen-year-old Lashai from London, whom I talked about in chapter 3: "My passion is my mission that my soul defines." To this day, those powerful words continue to resonate deep within my heart and soul.

EMBRACING YOUR PURPOSE

So how do you embrace your purpose? Here is a seven-step process that will help you complete this important part of self-care:

1. Get connected to your inner self, and the answers you are seeking will come. To live your life in divine purpose, start out by being quiet and listening to your inner voice, the spirit that lies deep within your soul.
2. Embrace the quiet moments by tapping into your deep beauty, which contains the essence of your personal values, passions, and strengths in the spirit of your virtue. You must be quiet and still to hear and listen to your inner voice, which will guide you to your purpose.
3. Be committed to listening to your inner voice. In sacred silence, you will find your peace, passion, and purpose. Just keep practicing your meditation.
4. Stay connected with like-minded people; listen to inspirational and spiritual experts. Also, it is of great benefit to study by reading, writing, and reciting. It a great and fun way to learn and grow.
5. Create a sacred place of silence. In meditating, select a consistent time so you can develop the habit of meditating daily. Find a quiet and comfortable space. Minimize light exposure.
6. When you are having an aha or defining moment, be sure to respond with action. If you don't write it down immediately or take action when your insights have arrived, you may miss a crucial opportunity.
7. Share love. Living in your purpose, you will discover the highest form of love and peace that resonates within your soul. In life, always share love.

I can't express enough the power of meditation. When you enter into your sacred place of silence, you will gain insights. In your sacred place of silence, you will get rid of the fears that have been holding you back and paralyzing your soul for years. Once you find and create your sacred place, you will start listening to your inner voice. In sacred silence, you will find your peace, passion, and purpose. Where there is peace, there is power.

I will forever believe that you do not have to find your purpose; your purpose will find you. Just stop, get out of your own way, and allow your God-given purpose and mission to come to you. Then you will get connected to your inner self, and the answers you are seeking will come. Your life purpose will unfold naturally and with ease; you never have to force it.

Why do I say that? When you start looking for your purpose, you may find yourself trying to pick and choose what you think your purpose should be. Often your purpose in life may not come close to what you may have imagined. Perhaps you are totally confused with your purpose because you are trying to duplicate someone else's gifts and or talents. Or perhaps you are blocking your purpose by practicing one or more of the following:

- Are you searching for the perfect purpose versus listening to your true calling?
- Do you dislike silence and need to be in a lot of noise?
- Are you afraid of being alone?
- Do you devalue the unconscious mind?

In my case, I spent many years of my adult life working as a clinical education manager. At that time, I thought I had found my niche in my career, and that it was my purpose. I was ready to spend the rest of my career doing what I went to school for, and I worked my way up through promotions. Then my life shifted to a greater calling that swiftly changed every plan and direction I had ever taken in my life. That was when the divine presence of light took my life on a different path for me to discover my real purpose. My genuine purpose came from the deep pain I experienced on September 19, 2007, when my father was having a massive subdural hematoma—that is, bleeding inside his skull was putting pressure on his brain. That was the day when I knew I needed to make a difference in the world.

I listened to my inner voice, which directed me to help family caregivers caring for their loved ones. I began working tirelessly toward improving and creating better laws for family caregivers. Without having any experience in book writing, I wrote my first book, *Why Wait? The Baby Boomers' Guide to Preparing Emotionally, Financially and Legally for a Parent's Death*, which at the time was the first book on the market about that subject.

And like always, my beloved father's voice stayed with me. One of his favorite readings helped me and continues to help me look at life with the proper perspective regarding purpose. I know that you are familiar with these words:

To everything, there is a season, a time for every purpose under heaven:
A time to be born, and a time to die; a time to plant, and a time to pluck
 what is planted;
A time to kill, and a time to heal; a time to break down, and a time to
 build up;

A time to weep, and a time to laugh; a time to mourn, and a time to dance;
A time to cast away stones, and a time to gather stones together; a time to embrace, and a time to refrain from embracing;
A time to get, and a time to lose; a time to keep, and a time to cast away;
A time to rend, and a time to sew; a time to keep silence, and a time to speak;
A time to love, and a time to hate; a time of war, and a time of peace.

(Ecclesiastes 3:1–8, KJV)

"LIVING YOUR PURPOSE" QUESTIONS

Now it's your time to pause and answer these questions. Before you answer, go to that place of quiet we have just talked about.

1. Do you know what your divine purpose is? Write it down as clearly as you can.
2. Have you ever had a deep sense about doing something great in your life, but you backed off? What was your reason?
3. What are your God-given gifts? List them.
4. Do you have a talent that you would like to share but haven't taken the time to embrace yet? Why?
5. Have you created a sacred place of silence in which to meditate? Where is it? If you have not, why not?
6. Have you ever sabotaged your gifts by pretending they don't exist?
7. Do you have any regrets for not following your heart? What is stopping you?

• *15* •

Why Giving Back to Others Is Essential

$\mathcal{T}$here is a Chinese saying that goes, "If you want happiness for an hour, take a nap. If you want happiness for a day, go fishing. If you want happiness for a year, inherit a fortune. If you want happiness for a lifetime, help somebody."[1]

I find true wisdom in these words. Helping others feeds the well of deep beauty and inner worth. Throughout my life, I have seen the transformation that occurs when people give back to others in both small and big ways. They don't expect a building to be named after them. They don't expect their businesses to profit. They don't expect any kind of reward. They give back. Period.

I have a dear friend named Marla who is one of the most beautiful and giving spirits I have ever known. A wife, mother of two, and grandmother, she also is the caregiver of her ninety-two-year-old mother, works full-time, and volunteers at our weekly meditation sessions.

Maria always has a sweet smile on her face no matter what she is going through. One day I asked her how she manages her busy life and still finds time to serve others. "Carolyn," she explained. "When I share love, the love that I get back is far greater than I can ever give. It settles and soothes my soul. I give love because it makes me feel good. I don't need to be recognized for doing it. The only thing I want and need in my life is to live a life of purpose, peace, and thanksgiving. Isn't that the way it's supposed to be?"

Such a sweet and simple answer! Let's hear some more stories and thoughts on giving back.

PURPOSE AND GIVING BACK

In the last chapter, we talked about purpose. Not surprisingly, many people's purpose is linked to making a difference in the world by helping others. Additionally, when you know your purpose in life, you experience a sense of urgency in wanting to give and help someone else in need. In turn, giving back can also help you achieve your purpose. When you give from the heart, you never know what blessings are in store and how many lives you are touching.

Here's my personal experience with this concept. As I have mentioned, one of my purposes in life is to help caregivers. In 2015 I was a guest on the *Good Life,* a television show where I talked about how caregivers could take better care of themselves. The producer of the show loved the passion I brought to the topic as well as the fact that ratings went through the roof. A few days later, the producer offered me a monthly twenty-minute segment on the show. *Across All Ages* was born, and it aired for fifteen months.

How did all of this happen? I firmly believe that when you know your purpose and help others, the universe will reward you more than you can ever imagine. When you give from your heart and soul, I assure you that your efforts will come back to you in so many ways that it is unbelievable. My dad once told me, "When you are called to do a mission, the commission will soon follow—just be patient."

GET MORE BY GIVING MORE

I firmly believe that some people may not see themselves as living in abundance. They can only see and focus on what's lacking in their lives. So they live a life of holding on tightly to everything, ultimately squeezing the giving experience out of every area of their life. Additionally, some people think that they don't have anything to offer, so they go through life not realizing that we are all born to contribute to the universe. If you give little portions, then expect only little portions to come back to you.

For an analogy, imagine scooping up a handful of sand on a beach. When you open your hand, you will keep at least 90 percent or more of the sand. However, once you close your hand and squeeze it tightly by making a fist, most of the sand will fall out of your grasp. It's just that simple. You get more when you are open to giving more.

Smart businesses know this. There is a pizza place in Baltimore called Joe Squared. Its owner, Joe Edwardsen, specifically put the restaurant in an urban area with many boarded-up buildings. For the last fifteen years, Joe Squared has been a stable force in the neighborhood and has served as an inspiration for many other businesses to open.

Under Joe's guidance, the restaurant sells the work of local artists and takes no commission, hosts local and regional bands and gives all ticket sales back to them, distributes pizza free to hundreds of organizations, and every month creates a special pizza in the name of a local nonprofit as a fundraiser. Additionally, the restaurant consciously hires and trains immigrants, artists, and other people who are trying to make a better life for their families.

One poignant moment took place in 2015 when there were protests in Baltimore. Joe Squared volunteers were out on the streets distributing free pizza to both the protesters and National Guard. A soldier who witnessed the calming of tempers as everyone sat down together to eat pizza described the moment as faith-restoring. He sent this email: "The world just needs more pizza."

Joe keeps quiet about giving back. He considers it boastful to toot his own horn. But the community recognizes that Joe Squared cares deeply about doing good and taking action. His customers and employees remain loyal, spread the word, and are the reason that Joe Squared has become a beloved institution in Baltimore.

In towns and cities across the world, business owners like Joe are improving the lives of people every day. They do it not to increase revenue but because they believe helping out is their responsibility and privilege. And as a result, their businesses thrive.

In addition, our world would come to a standstill without nonprofits. The engines that power nonprofits are volunteers and donations. With money and people, they accomplish things that are simply unbelievable.

While writing a check is important, I strongly urge you to give the gift of your time. It will transform your life. Here is a short list of community-based volunteer opportunities that I believe are well worth your while to become involved with:

1. Habitat for Humanity
2. American Red Cross
3. Girl Scouts and Boy Scouts
4. Kids against Hunger
5. Nursing Homes and Hospitals
6. Charity Sewing for Cancer Patients
7. Free Charity Sewing Projects for Shelters
8. Dress a Girl around the World
9. CareGiverStory Inc.

Also, the internet now opens up lots of opportunities for you to match causes you care about and your talents to organizations in need. Take a look at https://www.volunteermatch.org.

HEALTH BENEFITS OF VOLUNTEERING

While my view on giving back is that you should do it because it is the right thing to do, I have also been fascinated watching the health of my clients improve as they become more involved in volunteering their time. My observation has been supported by a significant amount of research.

A 2007 review of research titled *The Health Benefits of Volunteering* from the Office of Research and Policy Development, Corporation for National and Community Service, concluded:

> Over the past two decades we have seen a growing body of research that indicates volunteering provides individual health benefits in addition to social benefits. This research has established a strong relationship between volunteering and health: those who volunteer have lower mortality rates, greater functional ability, and lower rates of depression later in life than those who do not volunteer.
>
> Comparisons of the health benefits of volunteering for different age groups have also shown that older volunteers are the most likely to receive greater benefits from volunteering, whether because they are more likely to face higher incidence of illness or because volunteering provides them with physical and social activity and a sense of purpose at a time when their social roles are changing. Some of these findings also indicate that volunteers who devote a "considerable" amount of time to volunteer activities (about 100 hours per year) are most likely to exhibit positive health outcomes.[2]

TEACH YOUR CHILDREN WELL

Helping others also appears to cross generations within families. For example, Joe Edwardsen, whom I just talked about, had an eighty-six-year-old grandmother who volunteered sixty hours a week until she passed away. Joe's mother kept up the tradition with extensive mentoring and helping business owners at no charge. Now Joe continues the tradition of giving back through his restaurant.

Let me tell you one of my favorite stories about people who make giving back a core value in their families. Clover Reed lived in a small town in

Oklahoma. Her husband worked hard as a shoemaker and part-time minister in their community, but often their finances would come up a little short. A stay-at-home mom, Clover never stopped working hard, caring for their six children as well as being very active in her community.

One day a woman from her church stopped by the house with a basket full of dirty clothes. She explained that she didn't have time to wash them but to please clean them up and give the clothes to her growing children. She made the point that there were some beautiful items in the bottom of the basket.

Clover's youngest son was not happy. "Momma, why did you take the basket full of dirty clothes?" he asked. "I don't want to wear those clothes even after you have cleaned them."

A quiet and petite woman who stood only four feet and eleven inches tall, Clover admonished her son: "Henrey, you must learn to be grateful to anyone who shows you any act of kindness. At the bottom of the basket, there was a small white envelope with six $100 bills for each one of my kids. For if I had thrown away the basket full of dirty clothes, I would have thrown away the blessing to our family."

This is a true story about my Grandmother Clover Reed Brent and my Uncle Henrey. I learned several lessons from this story. First, it showed that sometimes you've got to take what you may not want to get the hidden treasures you can't see. Second, it reaffirmed that the legacy of helping others runs through my family into me. Third, it made me think about how we all develop into people of deep beauty and inner worth. The person you are today and the life you are living is a combination of many people and variables. We are the offspring of our parents, who give us life, as well as other folks who have poured into our life's experiences along the way.

We are molded by those who love and care about us. People who are bad for us and represent the ugly parts of life have also molded us. We *always* have the choice to become the person we want to be and live the life we want to have. People may mold us, but they never make us.

YOUR GIVING BACK CHECKLIST

Here is a simple checklist of ideas we have talked about in this chapter. How many of them can you make happen today as you transform your life? How many of them will make a sustainable impact on how you care for yourself?

✓ Create a positive difference in the world. Give of your time, skills, unique talents, or finances to make a lasting impact in someone's life.

Do so from the heart, without expecting anything in return. Offer your skills, such as creating newsletters or art, building social media platforms, or providing any form of technology services. Volunteer at a school. Call bingo numbers at a nursing home. Become a poetry reader in a group. Greet people at your place of worship. The list goes on and on.

✓ Strengthen your community. Whether you volunteer as a driver to transport your kids and their friends to school or volunteer to read stories at your local library, you will improve the community where you live, work, and enjoy recreation and relaxation. When you live in an active community, you will have a greater sense of security, health, and well-being for your family and those around you.

✓ Create new opportunities. When you offer to help a stranger, friend, and/or an organization, you never know what doors will open for you.

✓ Meet new people. Through volunteering, you will be amazed at the people you will meet. Volunteering is a delightful way to make new friends; you can talk to people who are relaxed and doing what they enjoy.

✓ Live your purpose. You are walking in your divine light. Your calling is a feeling and a fire in your heart and soul that you just can't shake away.

✓ Learn from others. Getting feedback from others is essential to learning and growing. Be observant. You can learn a lot by watching how someone with expertise approaches a situation.

✓ Feel blessed. Live a life of thanksgiving every day.

✓ Offer love. Love and kindness are great gifts to offer and they don't cost a dime.

✓ Forgive. Forgiving and letting go are acts of self-love; they free your soul.

✓ Say thank you. Saying thank you or sending a handwritten card goes a long way and makes a difference in someone else's life.

I'd like to conclude with a thank you to a special group of people. They don't get paid. They rarely take the time to enjoy a vacation. They often set aside their emotional, medical, financial, legal, and self-care needs. Who are these heroes? They are our family caregivers. I thank and salute you. You are the world's true heroes who demonstrate that true love is an act of giving unconditionally with no boundaries.

"WHY GIVING BACK TO OTHERS
IS ESSENTIAL" QUESTIONS

Now it's your time to pull out your binder or computer and think about and answer these questions:

1. What are your thoughts around giving?
2. Name the people in your life who have helped form your views on giving back to others? How did they impact you?
3. List a few new ways that you can give by actions other than writing a check.
4. When was the last time you sent a handwritten thank-you card to someone who made a difference in your life?
5. Have you considered volunteering in your community or for a national organization? If so, where, and when are you going to start?
6. Create a list of stuff in your home that you are no longer using, and then donate it to a cause that you are passionate about.

· *16* ·

What to Do When Your
Self-Care Engine Runs Dry

$\mathscr{T}$here will be times throughout your wellness self-care journey when you may get stuck, relapse, or go back to your old behaviors. A multitude of life's circumstances may derail you. There are challenges that can be triggered by factors like arguments with loved ones, employment issues, or addictive behaviors. Just know all of these are distractions that might take you off your new self-care routine, but there are ways to make sure these distractions are only temporary.

One thing people often say when they go off course is, "If only I had more willpower, then I would be able to. . . ." In my experience, this assessment ends up as an excuse not to refuel your self-care engine. Yes, willpower is important. However, you need to get at the reason why your willpower is waning as well as develop short- and long-term strategies that refill your willpower tank.

HOW WILLPOWER WORKS

Health writer Maia Szalavitz has examined research about why willpower often seems to fail us when we need it most. She explains, "Some researchers argue that willpower is a limited resource that wears out, like a muscle exhausted by overuse. Other experts say that our will may falter only if we think it's fallible: if we believe we have unlimited self-control, we do. The answer matters, of course, because the distinctly human capacity to temper one's impulses is essential to virtually all aspects of success."[1]

If you are facing a short-term challenge, you need to believe that your willpower is an unlimited resource that will get you through anything. Think of sprinters in a race. Those sprinters have only one focus: getting to the finish line as fast as they can. They need to completely believe that they have the willpower to make it happen.

Marathon runners, however, need to acknowledge that there are limits to willpower. They need to know how to pace themselves and not get distracted. They need to set up ways to keep themselves focused on the goal but allow for small rewards along the way to successfully complete the 26.2 miles. For example, experienced marathon runners often take a one-minute walking break every eight minutes to recover. This strategy is viewed as more effective in giving them a faster time than plowing through with sheer willpower.

Additionally, there have been countless studies that look at self-discipline and achieving goals. Results are inconclusive as to why some people have more self-discipline than others. However, one theme does emerge: limiting exposure to distractions is useful in improving willpower. This does not mean spending all your energy resisting temptation but rather creating an environment that reduces exposure to things that drain you.

What does that mean for you? If the people surrounding you are negative and practice overindulgence, then you are living in an environment that will eventually drain your willpower. If eating out is your main source of recreation and a daily occurrence, then you will have more challenges creating a successful environment for maintaining a healthy food plan. If your life is completely off balance with too much stress and work, then practicing self-care will become more difficult.

So the first thing you need to do when you feel your self-care engine is running dry is to stop and assess what is going on. You can't just power through it with willpower. You need to find where the block, distraction, or disconnect is in order to find out why you are going off course.

The key is never to beat yourself up. You need to acknowledge that you are just passing through a temporary rough patch. Just recognize you need to stop, assess, and recharge your self-care engine.

STOP, ASSESS, AND RECHARGE YOUR SELF-CARE ENGINE

One of my inspirations for the stop, assess, and recharge strategy is my dear friend David, a two-time cancer survivor. He is a walking miracle who exemplifies taking action after getting knocked down. I asked him how he manages to get his self-care back on track when he's had so many life-threatening health concerns.

"When you are that sick, you start putting your life in the proper perspectives," he said. "I've learned to stay focused on my life's real meaning, mission, and purpose. My cancer and surviving it has made me laser-focused on self-care and helping others that are experiencing the same things I have.

"Cancer is all around us in the way we think; some of the internal feelings or someone's attitude can be as deadly as cancer. And any contrary events around you can mimic a cancer if you allow them in your life."

Today, David shares his inspirational story as he travels nationally teaching people how to get back on track on their self-care journey and get focused on the great things that really matters in life. He explains, "Carolyn, I was blessed to be healed of my cancer. I made a promise to God that I would help others, and I've been delivered from my illness."[2]

As you can see, David is a thinker and a doer. Facing cancer, he went through obstacles by looking at his attitude, staying focused, believing in God, and taking action as he sought healing. While his story may be more dramatic, every day we are faced with challenges that can cause our self-care engine to sputter and even shut down.

Let's take a look at Janet, a busy single parent who is raising two kids, finishing a degree, and working part time. Her children—six-year-old Jamie and eight-year-old Matthew—are the most important part of her life. She is also focused on losing forty pounds since she is not happy about how she looks or feels.

Janet worked with me and implemented a blood type eating plan and a body type exercise plan. She was getting results and had lost twenty pounds. One day she came to me and said she was going to stop because she had too much on her plate. One child had piano lessons. Another was taking dance classes. And she had volunteered to head a Boy Scout troop because no one else would step up. "My stress level is at an all-time high," she said, "and I just don't have time or the energy involved with doing meal planning and exercising."

I asked her not to make a decision but rather to take a week off from her self-care program. During that time, I requested that she use one hour a day to look over her journals, relax, and think about why she wanted to get healthier in the first place.

She came back to me the following week with an aha moment. She said that she realized that since one of her primary whys for practicing self-care was to be healthier for her children, she could not put her own program on the back burner. She wanted to be in the best possible physical and emotional state as she raised them. So together we worked on strategies to help her continue her self-care program. She engaged her support network to help with food shopping and preparation and switched to a gym that had a great program for kids so she could exercise while they were having fun.

She also acknowledged that to some extent she was using her kids as an excuse to not continuing on with her goal of losing twenty more pounds. She realized that this was actually a pattern in her life. She would lose half the weight, feel better, and then stop before reaching her goal. She then would feel bad about not reaching her goal and put the weight back on.

We recalibrated her thinking away from weight and more around honoring a daily commitment. Each day she would eat according to her food plan. Each day she would practice meditation. Each day she would do physical activity. She would no longer be focused on the scale; instead she would be focused on making each day count toward self-care. And we decided to give her one day off each week if she wanted to not commit to her plan.

Today, Janet has lost forty pounds and kept it off for eighteen months. She feels emotionally more stable and physically at the top of her game. "The thing I am probably the most proud of is the example I am setting for my children," she says. "They ask for a lot less junk food than before and will play outside instead of watching television. They are happier, and that makes me happier too."

And interestingly enough, after the first month back, she did not take off the one day a week that we had planned for. She liked keeping to her plan every day. It made her feel in charge and successful. She liked the way her body and mind felt keeping a daily routine and not indulging in her old behaviors.

TWENTY STRATEGIES TO REFUEL YOUR SELF-CARE ENGINE

Janet and I incorporated several strategies to refuel her engine. They are included in the following list of twenty strategies I have put together for you based on my experience with hundreds of clients. Use whichever ones are helpful to reboot your wellness journey and get back on track. If one doesn't help, select another. *They work, and you can do it.*

1. When your self-care engine is running low or there's no more gas, then acknowledge that this is a normal occurrence. It is healthy for you to recognize when you need a break. Think about it: even machines break down and require a reboot.
2. Read the answers to the questions in this book that you have written in your journal. They will remind you of where you have been, where you want to go, and how you are going to get there.
3. If you get disheartened because you are not seeing results at first, enact strategies to counteract discouragement. Talk to a friend. Revisit your mission. Meditate on patience.

4. If you stop for a couple of days because of something in your life, start over quickly. The more time you let lapse, the harder it will be.

5. If your partner or family is not supportive, don't let this stop you. You are your own true love. They don't need to join you, but do not let them stand in your way.

6. Achieve clarity of the mind by permitting yourself not to think about anything that is unsettling to your soul. Do not force your mind to push through difficult situations or deal with troublesome issues that are out of your control. Let go.

7. Allow yourself to do something fun: small treats that will not actually get in the way of your goals.

8. Rest. Simply do nothing; just rest. Incorporate activities of relaxation for your mind, body, and spirit. Take long walks on the beach. Garden. Enjoy bubble baths.

9. Know that your thoughts are powerful. Practice the affirmations we have talked about in this book.

10. Plan "me time." Try aiming for at least an hour per day. You can take your time at once or divide that hour into small intervals that work best for you.

11. Find a quiet place just for you. It could be in your home, library, or anywhere that provides solitude and relaxation. Once you find that place, start focusing on your inner thoughts by going deep beneath the surface of what's happening around you.

12. Surround yourself with positivity. Turn off the news. Visit good friends. Watch cat videos if they make you happy. Read an inspirational book.

13. Revisit your why. Remember the reason why you really want to get healthy.

14. Acknowledge your truth. It is essential for you to acknowledge and be truthful about where your health is now. Look at how far you have come, but look at the truth of where you are. Is your blood pressure still too high? Are you still filled with anxiety? Have you gotten back into a bad relationship? Are you relying on buying things to make you feel good?

15. Stop looking for excuses. Remember that you have the ability to re-engage your made-up-mind attitude by transforming your thoughts into a can-do, winning mindset.

16. Resist temptation. When you resist one temptation, chances are you have a better chance to withstand the next temptation more easily.

17. Avoid being around anything that may trigger any past addictions, such as any old behavior of overindulging in food, sugar, alcohol, and drugs.

18. Ask yourself again what you are willing to do to succeed. Are you willing to commit more time? Are you up to reading more books? Do you need to seek professional guidance? When you genuinely want to succeed, you will do what it takes.

19. Keep your commitments. If you have committed to eating according to your blood type, do it. If you have committed to exercising three times a day, do it. Look at your self-care commitments as the same kind of commitments you would make to your loved ones. Would you not show up for your child's soccer practice if he was counting on you? Would you not take your mother to a doctor's appointment? Would you forget your husband's birthday?

20. Remember that greatness takes time. Mediate on patience. Measure the small successes. Get clearly in touch with how your body is feeling so you recognize improvement.

"WHAT TO DO WHEN YOUR SELF-CARE ENGINE RUNS DRY" QUESTIONS

Now it's your time pull out your binder or computer and think about and answer these questions:

1. Why do you think your self-care engine is running dry? When did you recognize it?

2. Are you having a challenge with an old behavior or temptation? If so, how are you managing it? Do you need to speak with your trusted healthcare professional? If so, when do you plan to make the call?

3. Are you feeling down or depressed? If so, what are you doing to manage your feelings? Have you spoken to your trusted healthcare professional yet? If so, what were the recommendations? If you haven't spoken to anyone, when do you plan to do so?

4. Have you thought about taking some time off for relaxation, meditation, a therapeutic bubble bath, or something similar? If you haven't, what's stopping you?

5. How do you plan to reboot your self-care engine? When do you feel that you will be ready to start? Write down your start date.

· 17 ·

Rejoicing in Your Life

*W*e have reached the end of this stage of your self-care journey: reading this book. At this point, I hope you are excited about what you need to do to bring self-care into your life. I hope you truly believe that this will be a transforming experience. I hope you will see self-care as very doable, no matter where you are currently in your life.

I also hope that you believe—as I do—that we are all born with unique gifts to serve. Only you know deep in your soul what contributions you will make and your purpose for being born. Just trust that you are divinely protected, safe, and secure all within yourself. Believe and hold on to your God-given purpose and mission.

What I want you to do right now is to rejoice in your deep beauty and inner worth. Say it as your new affirmation:

> I rejoice in my deep beauty.
> I rejoice in my inner worth.
> I rejoice in my life.

Didn't that feel good? As I have said throughout this book, words have power. Remember that when we talked about transformation, I said that true transformation requires the structure and control that makes you repeatedly do what needs to be done to achieve your goals, no matter if they are personal or professional.

Remember my definition of *self-care*: loving yourself. It involves reminding yourself that you are important and then following through with consistent action. It is about putting yourself first and understanding that you cannot care for others unless you care for yourself.

And remember the power in the words "deep beauty" and "inner worth." Deep beauty comes from a heart, soul, mind, and body that are joyous, grateful, and generous. It comes from truly enjoying life on a cellular level. It comes from working hard to be the absolute best you can be and then sharing that experience with others. It is about knowing your inner worth.

So why is "rejoice" such an important word? Rejoicing means to feel or show great joy or delight. It is about happiness, delight, and celebration. Too often in our world we forget about rejoicing in our life. We get so caught up in the mundane that we forget the profound: we are alive and life is a gift.

As my own trainer, Jocelyn, shares about rejoicing, "I rejoice when I get out of the bed and put my feet on the floor. That is when I rejoice, because I am alive, healthy, and blessed to be on this side of the ground."

I have had the incredible honor of meeting incredible people who rejoice in their lives. All of them have transformed their lives through self-care. All are committed to helping others, just as I know you will help others as you embrace your deep beauty and self-worth.

Their stories cross all ages, spiritual beliefs, and cultural backgrounds. The common denominator is that they demonstrate that when you rejoice daily, you will discover that the highest form of love and peace is within you. Let me share some of their stories and words with you.

CHRISTINE: THE ART OF MOTHERHOOD

Christine Jackson is a single mother of two boys, ages fourteen and fifteen, one of whom has special needs and requires specialized care. She also is an International Federation of Bodybuilding and Fitness professional, personal fitness coach, and motivational speaker. She helps other parents who have children with special needs to take care of themselves. She helps her clients transform their bodies and attitudes by rejoicing daily and embracing the life they were blessed with.

I asked Christine how she manages to be a supermom who understands life's challenges and thrives regardless of circumstances. "Carolyn, it is my deep-rooted faith, unwavering Christian beliefs. I rejoice daily and I am thankful to have been blessed with two amazing sons," she says. "The love I have for my sons gives me the strength, stamina, and grace that I need to raise my boys in a loving and empowering environment."

ZULIETH: MAKING HER YOUNG VOICE HEARD

Zulieth is tiny and young but a rising entrepreneur playing in the big pond of South Florida. In high school, she was a Silver Knight recipient, joining a select group of outstanding students who excelled in academic and community service.

Health is at the forefront of her life. She is a practicing vegetarian, an avid gym-goer, a lover of outdoor activities, and a frequent meditator. She believes in the power of information, education, and community service. She lives her life by three rules:

1. Be kind. Stand for the weak, the sick, and the unseen, for they too have a say in our future.
2. Know that quality and equal access to education for all is the bridge that carries a society to the next level of greatness.
3. Get informed, stay connected, and vote in every election, local or national, no matter how small. Your voice and your vote can change the world.

BEN: SHARING HIS MESSAGE AROUND THE WORLD

Ben delivered his first message in third grade as a child prodigy. He started a weekly home Bible study at age 16, and became a full-time pastor in his senior year of high school. He is always encouraging and inspiring humans from every walk of life to never ever give up because, he says, "If you've got a pulse, you've got a purpose. So rejoice."

At twenty-eight, Ben believes that rejoicing daily is good for the mind, body and soul. A gifted and nationally renowned speaker, author, and host of a national radio program, his energy, humor, and uplifting style touch the lives of thousands of people as he travels across the world.

Today he reaches across the board with the message God has put in his heart: "Now may the God of hope fill you all with joy and peace in believing, that you may abound in hope by the power of the Holy Spirit" (Romans 15:13).

DEBORAH: MAKING HER WORLD BIGGER

At sixty-five, Deborah has experienced a lot of life: Woodstock and protests in the '60s, burying one husband and divorcing two others, raising sons into amazing fathers and husbands, working for large corporations, starting her own companies, living with people with serious drug addictions; and a host of other life experiences.

As she ages, Deborah remembers the contrast between her own mother and aunt as they aged. Her mother's world became bigger. She volunteered and surrounded herself with young people. She traveled whenever and wherever she could. She loved life even as her body started breaking down.

Her aunt's world became very small. A widow at a young age who also lost her daughter, she rarely left her apartment and did not make new friends because she was scared of experiencing loss again. Until she passed away in her '90s, her attitude became more bitter with each year.

Deborah has consciously chosen to be like her mother. She travels, dances, and makes new friends at a drop of a hat. She keeps working because she loves what she does and volunteers whenever she can. There are simply not enough hours in the day for her to do everything she wants.

Now at sixty-five, she is on her own self-care journey. "I rejoice in living every day and know that to continue having adventures and satisfying my curiosity, I need to stay as healthy as I can."

ANGELA: FAMILY FIRST

Angela is a woman of faith, and she rejoices every day as she thinks about her strong family legacy and what the word "family" truly means to her. When Angela was only thirteen months old, her mother passed away suddenly and unexpectedly. Her mother's siblings stepped in and raised Angela as their own.

Thirty years later, Angela raised her niece and nephew due to the passing of their mother. Angela believes strongly in family bonds and rejoices daily to have been blessed with a great family.

I asked Angela how she stayed motivated. She replied, "Carolyn, I am living a purpose-filled life, and I recognize that who I am today is a result of my aunties, uncles, nieces, nephews, brothers, sisters, and extended family that has helped create the woman I am."

MY "NOR WOULD I" LIST

When I began to walk in the light of my divine purpose, I felt in my heart that I was on my spiritual journey. At the time, I had no idea where it was guiding me. I only knew I had to follow the deep passion that was in my heart and soul regarding helping those without a voice. When I started serving others, my pain began to dissolve.

While on my journey, I walked through a lot of peaks and valleys. Yes, I climbed some unbelievable mountains in my life, but I never looked at how high I had to climb to reach the mountaintop. When you are living your life with a purpose and on a mission, you are just driven to do the work. And you trust that God will take you to the top of the mountain in victory.

Has my spiritual journey been hard? My answer is that it's a lot of work, yet it comprises the deepest, most significant, and remarkable experiences I have ever known. I am still speechless when I stop and think about the miracles of where people's spiritual journeys have taken them.

But what if I would have ignored my calling? What if I had given up? This is my "I would not have" rejoice list of the miracles in my life. If I hadn't walked in my purpose and followed my divine light,

- Nor would I have known what an amazing gift it was for me to be of service to represent those without a voice. It gives my soul unimaginable serenity and peace.
- Nor would I have embraced the significant power of what forgiveness brings, how it frees my soul, and how to trust and love again.
- Nor would I have known to incorporate self-care by tapping into my deep beauty and inner worth.
- Nor would I have discovered how to become healthier and live a life of wellness, peace, happiness, purpose, and rejoicing.

Just creating the "nor would I" list brings unbelievable tears of joy to my eyes. Because too often you don't see what you have accomplished until you stop and write about it. Then you rejoice from the bottom of your soul.

I urge all of you to write down your "nor would I" list. I urge all of you to listen to the stories of other people. Most of all, I urge you to love yourself through discipline, action, and determination. I end with a favorite quote from an unknown writer:

> "An empty lantern provides no light. Self-care is
> the fuel that allows your light to shine brightly."

"REJOICING IN YOUR LIFE" QUESTIONS

Answer these final questions, and make sure you refer back to your journal often.

1. Do you rejoice daily? Create a list of what rejoicing does for you.
2. Where do you believe your spiritual journey is guiding you?
3. Create a list of the miracles you have experienced by transforming your life through self-care by tapping into your deep beauty and inner worth.

Notes

INTRODUCTION

1. Wilhelm Hofman, Maike Luhmann, Rachel R. Fisher, Kathleen D. Vohs, and Roy F. Baumeister "Yes, But Are They Happy? Effects of Trait Self-Control on Affective Well-Being and Life Satisfaction," *Journal of Personality*, 82: 4 August 2014, https://onlinelibrary.wiley.com/doi/epdf/10.1111/jopy.12050?referrer_access_token -VYpCM2wGndCJqmYZilGMtYta6bR2k8jH0KrdpFOxC64ZkFBdIIHYL CNufdlB4xyAtl9yP9ZtcXvPx_xya63FhwmUKHtB-ODxLMBsZMSVQwxG -U2ASFxvMgPzK2V8II393

CHAPTER 3: WHEN AHA MOMENTS BECOME DEFINING MOMENTS

1. David Rock and Josh Davis, "4 Steps to Having More 'Aha' Moments" *Harvard Business Review*, October 12, 2016, https://hbr.org/2016/10/4-steps-to-having -more-aha-moments.

2. "Scientists Explain 'Aha!' Moments," WebMD, April 13, 2004, https://www .webmd.com/men/news/20040413/scientists-explain-aha-moments.

3. E. J. Masicampo and Roy F. Baumeister, "Consider It Done! Plan Making Can Eliminate the Cognitive Effects of Unfulfilled Goals," *Journal of Personality and Social Psychology*, June 20, 2011, doi:10.1037/a0024192.

4. Alice Boyes, "15 Psychology Experts Share Their Personal 'Aha' Moments," *Psychology Today*, February 25, 2013, https://www.psychologytoday.com/us/blog/ in-practice/201302/15-psychology-experts-share-their-personal-aha-moments.

5. Georges Bernanos, BrainyQuote, https://www.brainyquote.com/quotes/georges _bernanos_135466.

CHAPTER 4: WHY WE RESIST SELF-CARE

1. Anna Medaris Miller, "No Spouse, No Kids, No Caregiver: How to Prepare to Age Alone, U.S. News & World Report," October 26, 2015, https://health.usnews.com/health-news/health-wellness/articles/2015/10/26/no-spouse-no-kids-no-caregiver-how-to-prepare-to-age-alone.

2. Kerry Justich, "80-Year-Old Body Builder: 'Age is Nothing but a Number,'" Yahoo Lifestyle, June 20, 2016, https://www.yahoo.com/lifestyle/80-old-fitness-trainer-prove-000000042.html.

3. Lorraine C. Ladish, "This Latina Bodybuilder Is 71: 'We Should Never Give Up on Ourselves,'" CBS News, July 24, 2017, https://www.nbcnews.com/news/latino/latina-bodybuilder-71-we-should-never-give-ourselves-n786051.

4. Ralph Ryback, "Why We Resist Change," *Psychology Today*, January 25, 2017, https://www.psychologytoday.com/us/blog/the-truisms-wellness/201701/why-we-resist-change.

5. Ibid.

6. Monica A. Frank and Susan Gustafson, "Exercise and the Self-Esteem Cycle," Excel at Life, https://www.excelatlife.com/articles/selfesteemexercise.htm.

7. Ronald Alexander, "The Power of Affirmations: How to Make Them Work for You," HuffPost, updated October 9, 2011, https://www.huffingtonpost.com/ronald-alexander-phd/positive-affirmations_b_921184.html.

8. Joel Brown, "34 Inspirational Quotes by Wayne Dyer," Addicted2Success, July 10, 2014, https://addicted2success.com/quotes/34-wayne-dyer-quotes-that-will-inspire-success-in-you.

CHAPTER 5: RECLAIMING YOUR HEALTH

1. Jesus Jimenez, "10 Unforgettable Quotes," *Success Magazine*, September 2014, https://www.success.com/article/10-unforgettable-quotes-by-jim-rohn.

2. Katherine DeClerq, "In Maya Angelou's Words: 'All Great Achievements Require Time,'" CTVNews.ca, May 28, 2014, https://www.ctvnews.ca/mobile/entertainment/in-maya-angelou-s-words-all-great-achievements-require-time-1.1842120.

CHAPTER 6: WHAT REALLY HAPPENS AS WE AGE

1. Scott LaFee, "Aging Casefully: 9 Things That Happen to Your Body (Some Aren't So Bad!)," *UC San Diego Health News*, August 2015.

2. Mark E. Williams, "How Does Our Body Change as We Age? The Art and Science of Aging Well," *Psychology Today*, May 2017.

3. "Osteoporosis and Asian American Women," National Institute of Arthritis and Musculoskeletal and Skin Diseases, https://www.bones.nih.gov/health-info/bone/osteoporosis/background/asian-american-women.

4. Hannah Nichols, "What Happens to the Brain as We Age?" MedicalNewsToday, August 2017, https://www.medicalnewstoday.com/articles/319185.php.

5. Emily Rogalski, "Cognitive Aging Summit III, Neurobiological Features of SuperAgers," https://www.youtube.com/watch?v=8_xu8uYMVEg.

6. Robert Waldinger, "What Makes a Good Life? Lessons from the Longest Study on Happiness," TED, https://www.ted.com/talks/robert_waldinger_what_makes _a_good_life_lessons_from_the_longest_study_on_happiness.

7. "The 90+ Study," UCI Mind, http://www.mind.uci.edu/research-studies/90plus -study.

8. Edward Group, "The Health Benefits of Olive Oil," Global Healing Center, June 2014, https://www.globalhealingcenter.com/natural-health/benefits-of-olive-oil.

CHAPTER 7: WHY DISCIPLINE IS IMPORTANT

1. Bethany Brookshire, "Scientists Say: Neurotransmitters," *Science News for Students*, November 9, 2015, https://www.sciencenewsforstudents.org/blog/scientists -say/scientists-say-neurotransmitters.

2. Hara Estroff Marano, "Emotional Discipline," *Psychology Today*, June 9, 2016, https://www.psychologytoday.com/us/articles/200304/emotional-discipline.

CHAPTER 8: BLOOD TYPES
AND YOUR IMMUNE SYSTEM

1. "Lupus Facts and Statistics," National Resource Center on Lupus, 2018, https://resources.lupus.org/entry/facts-and-statistics.

2. JoAnn Manson, Eric Rimm, and Frank Hu, "Blood Type Linked to Heart Disease Risk," Harvard School of Public Health, August 14, 2012, https://www.hsph .harvard.edu/news/hsph-in-the-news/qi-blood-type-heart-disease-risk.

3. Peter D'Adamo, *Eat Right for Your Type* (New York: Putnam: 1996).

4. John Briffa, "No Evidence for the 'Blood Type Diet', but Does It Work?" drbriffa: A Good Look at Good Health, June 3, 2013, http://www.drbriffa.com/ 2013/06/03/no-evidence-for-the-blood-type-diet-but-does-it-work.

5. Mayo Clinic Staff, "Food Allergy," Mayo Clinic, April 2, 2017, https://www .mayoclinic.org/diseases-conditions/food-allergy/symptoms-causes/syc-20355095.

6. "Common Food Allergy Triggers," WebMD, https://www.webmd.com/allergies/ food-triggers#1.

CHAPTER 9: DEVELOPING YOUR OWN MEAL PLAN

1. "Harmful, Fake Health Foods," Advanced Plan for Health, July 24, 2018, http://www.mypoindexter.com/index.cfm/news-events/blog/harmful-fake-health-foods.

2. Dr. Mercola, "Here's What Eating Nothing but McDonalds for 10 Days Does to Your Gut Bacteria," Mercola: Take Control of your Health, May 27, 2015, https://articles.mercola.com/sites/articles/archive/2015/05/27/processed-foods-gut -microbes.aspx.

3. Corey Pemberton, "7 Signs Your Gut Bacteria Are Out of Whack," Paleo-hacks, https://blog.paleohacks.com/7-signs-your-gut-bacteria-are-out-of-whack.

4. Evelyn Lewin, "How Preservatives Can Make Us Gain Weight," *Sydney Morning Herald*, August 19, 2017, https://www.smh.com.au/lifestyle/health-and -wellness/how-preservatives-can-make-us-gain-weight-20170818-gxz28b.html.

5. Hrefna Palsdottir, "Does Junk Food Slow Down Your Metabolism?" HealthLine, March 21, 2017, https://www.healthline.com/nutrition/junk-food-and -metabolism#section2.

6. Christopher J. L. Murray, Marie Ng, and Ali Mokdad, "The Vast Majority of American Adults Are Overweight or Obese, and Weight Is a Growing Problem among US Children," Institute for Health Metrics and Evaluation (IHME), http://www.healthdata.org/news-release/vast-majority-american-adults-are-overweight-or -obese-and-weight-growing-problem-among.

7. Admin, "Essential Cultures Probiotics Leaf Origin Review," Healthy Nutrition Diets, January 12, 2016, http://www.healthynutritiondiets.com/probiotics/ essential-cultures-probiotics-leaf-origin-reviews.

8. Annie Price, "Lipase: The Digestive Enzyme that Fights Major Diseases," Dr. Axe, https://draxe.com/lipase.

9. Erica Kannall, "Role of Amylase," SFGATE, http://healthyeating.sfgate.com/ role-amylase-8526.html.

10. Dr. Mercola, "Bromelain Can Help Abate Inflammation," Mercola: Take Control of Your Health, https://articles.mercola.com/vitamins-supplements/bromelain .aspx.

11. Dana Leigh Smith, "30 Worst Foods for Your Heart," Eat This, Not That, May 25, 2018, https://www.eatthis.com/foods-that-cause-heart-disease.

12. Leslie Beck, "Top 25 Foods for Longevity, *Globe and Mail*, updated April 30, 2018, https://www.theglobeandmail.com/life/health-and-fitness/top-25-foods-for -longevity/article560323.

13. Editors of Rodale.com, "Top 12 Disease-Fighting Foods," *ABC Good Morning America*, https://abcnews.go.com/Health/Wellness/top-12-disease-fighting-foods/ story?id=17886289.

14. J. D. Cameron, M. J. Cyr, and E. Doucet, "Increased Meal Frequency Does Not Promote Greater Weight Loss in Subjects Who Were Prescribed an 8-Week Equi-Energetic Energy-Restricted Diet," PubMed.gov, https://www.ncbi.nlm.nih .gov/pubmed/19943985.

CHAPTER 10: HOW TO EXERCISE FOR YOUR BODY TYPE AND ABILITIES

1. "The Secret to Better Health—Exercise," Harvard Health Publishing, https://www.health.harvard.edu/healthbeat/the-secret-to-better-health-exercise.
2. "What Your Body Shape Says about Your Health," WebMD, https://www.webmd.com/diet/ss/slideshow-body-shape-health.
3. Joel Snape, "Ectomorph, Endomorph and Mesomorph: How to Train for Your Body Type," Coach, September 1, 2017, http://www.coachmag.co.uk/lifestyle/4511/ectomorph-endomorph-or-mesomorph-what-is-your-body-type.
4. "What Your Body Shape Says About Your Health."
5. "The Importance of Matching Exercises to Your Body Type," Ufiit by Adrianne, https://ufiit.com/the-importance-of-matching-exercises-to-your-body-type.
6. Sports Medicine, "What Your Body Shape Says about Your Health," UPMC, September 1, 2015, https://share.upmc.com/2015/09/what-body-shape-says-about-health-infographic.
7. Jenna Fletcher, "Six Sciatica Stretches for Pain Relief," MedicalNewsToday, June 14, 2017, https://www.medicalnewstoday.com/articles/317920.php.
8. "7 Stretching & Strengthening Exercises for a Frozen Shoulder," Harvard Health Publishing, updated November 29, 2017, https://www.health.harvard.edu/shoulders/stretching-exercises-frozen-shoulder.
9. David Heitz and Erica Cirino, "6 Stretches for Sciatica Pain Relief," Healthline, https://www.healthline.com/health/back-pain/sciatic-stretches.
10. Amy Rutherford-Close, "7 Exercises to Improve Balance," Active, https://www.active.com/fitness/articles/7-exercises-to-improve-balance?page=2.

CHAPTER 11: DEALING WITH STRESS

1. Christian Nordqvist, "Why Stress Happens and How to Manage It," MedicalNewsToday, November 28, 2017, https://www.medicalnewstoday.com/articles/145855.php.

CHAPTER 12: INCORPORATING MEDITATION INTO SELF-CARE

1. "Meditation: In Depth," National Center for Complementary and Integrative Health, https://nccih.nih.gov/health/meditation/overview.htm.
2. Alice G. Walton, "Different Types of Meditation Change Different Areas of the Brain, Study Finds," *Forbes*, October 5, 2017, https://www.forbes.com/

sites/alicegwalton/2017/10/05/different-types-of-meditation-change-the-brain-in
-different-ways-study-finds/#e4168f61f1ea.

3. Mindworks Team, "Meditation Definition: What Is Meditation?" Mindworks, https://mindworks.org/meditation-knowledge/meditation-definition-what
-is-meditation.

4. Mindworks Team, "How Many People Meditate?" Mindworks, https://
mindworks.org/meditation-knowledge/how-many-people-meditate.

5. Mindworks Team, "How Many People Meditate?" Mindworks, https://mind-
works.org/meditation-knowledge/how-many-people-meditate.

6. Giovanni, "Master Your Mind, Master Your Life," Live and Dare, last reviewed
July 6, 2018 https://liveanddare.com/types-of-meditation.

7. Yoga International, "What Are the 7 Chakras?" Yoga International, https://
yogainternational.com/article/view/what-are-the-7-chakras.

8. Sonia Jones, "A Mindful Eating Meditation to Manage Food Cravings," *Yoga
Journal*, January 26, 2015, https://www.yogajournal.com/lifestyle/mindful-eating
-meditation-manage-food-cravings.

CHAPTER 13: THE REAL CONNECTION
BETWEEN HEALTH AND MONEY

1. April Dykman, The Financial Cost of Obesity, Get Rich Slowly, July 2011,
https://www.getrichslowly.org/the-financial-cost-of-obesity/.

2. Kirsten Weir, "The Power of Self-Control," American Psychological Association, January 2012, http://www.apa.org/monitor/2012/01/self-control.aspx.

3. Luvleen Sidhu, "Health Is Wealth: How Good Health Can Increase Your Net
Worth," Popsugar Living, September 12, 2017, https://www.popsugar.com/career/
Connection-Between-Money-Health-43615325.

4. Ibid.

5. Ibid.

6. Ibid.

7. Phoebe Venable, "Your Health and Financial Wealth Are Closely Linked,"
Tennessean, August 22, 2014, https://amp.tennessean.com/amp/14462223.

8. Elsevier Health Sciences, "Over 60 Percent of All US Bankruptcies Attributable to Medical Problems," *Sciences Daily*, June 5, 2009, https://www.sciencedaily
.com/releases/2009/06/090604095123.htm.

9. Dave Ramsey, "7 Baby Steps," Ramsey Solutions, https://www.daveramsey
.com/baby-steps.

10. By Rachel Cruze, How to Make a Zero-Based Budget, Dave Ramsey, https://
www.daveramsey.com/blog/how-to-make-a-zero-based-budget.

11. Dave Ramsey, "Learn How to Budget," Ramsey Solutions, 2018, https://www
.daveramsey.com/budgeting/how-to-budget.

12. How to Get Out of Debt With the Debt Snowball Plan, Dave Ramey, Ramsey
Solutions 2018, https://www.daveramsey.com/blog/get-out-of-debt-with-the-debt
-snowball-plan.

CHAPTER 14: LIVING YOUR PURPOSE

1. Bronnie Ware, "Top 5 Regrets of The Dying," HuffPost, March 2, 2013, https://www.huffingtonpost.com/bronnie-ware/top-5-regrets-of-the-dyin_b_1220965.html.
2. Brainy Quote | Maria Shriver Quotes, https://www.brainyquote.com/quotes/maria_shriver_553677.
3. Joel Brown, "34 Inspirational Wayne Dyer Quotes," Quotes, July 10, 2014, https://addicted2success.com/quotes/34-wayne-dyer-quotes-that-will-inspire-success-in-you.

CHAPTER 15: WHY GIVING BACK TO OTHERS IS ESSENTIAL

1. Jenny Santi, "The Secret to Happiness Is Helping Others," *Time*, August 4, 2017, http://time.com/collection/guide-to-happiness/4070299/secret-to-happiness.
2. Corporation for National and Community Service, Office of Research and Policy Development, *The Health Benefits of Volunteering: A Review of Recent Research* (Washington, DC, 2007), https://www.nationalservice.gov/sites/default/files/documents/07_0506_hbr.pdf.

CHAPTER 16: WHAT TO DO WHEN YOUR SELF-CARE ENGINE RUNS DRY

1. Maia Szalavitz, "Improving Willpower: How to Keep Self-Control from Flagging," *Time*, September 19, 2012, http://healthland.time.com/2012/09/19/improving-willpower-how-to-keep-self-control-from-flagging.
2. Rodolfo Roman, "Cancer Survivor Hopes to Complete Documentary about His Two-Time Fight with Disease," *Miami Herald*, November 16, 2015, https://www.miamiherald.com/living/health-fitness/article45118308.html.

Bibliography

Admin. "Essential Cultures Probiotics Leaf Origin Review." Healthy Nutrition Diets. January 12, 2016. http://www.healthynutritiondiets.com/probiotics/essential -cultures-probiotics-leaf-origin-reviews.

Alexander, Ronald. "The Power of Affirmations: How to Make Them Work for You." HuffPost. Updated October 9, 2011. https://www.huffingtonpost.com/ ronald-alexander-phd/positive-affirmations_b_921184.html.

Beck, Leslie. "Top 25 Foods for Longevity." *Globe and Mail.* Updated April 30, 2018. https://www.theglobeandmail.com/life/health-and-fitness/top-25-foods-for -longevity/article560323.

Bernanos, Georges. BrainyQuote. https://www.brainyquote.com/quotes/georges _bernanos_135466.

Boyes, Alice. "15 Psychology Experts Share Their Personal 'Aha' Moments." *Psychology Today,* February 25, 2013. https://www.psychologytoday.com/us/blog/in -practice/201302/15-psychology-experts-share-their-personal-aha-moments.

Briffa, John. "No Evidence for the 'Blood Type Diet,' but Does It Work?" drbriffa: A Good Look at Good Health. June 3, 2013. http://www.drbriffa.com/2013/06/03/ no-evidence-for-the-blood-type-diet-but-does-it-work.

Brookshire, Bethany. "Scientists Say: Neurotransmitters." *Science News for Students.* November 9, 2015. https://www.sciencenewsforstudents.org/blog/scientists-say/ scientists-say-neurotransmitters.

Brown, Joel. "34 Inspirational Wayne Dyer Quotes." Addicted2Success. July 10, 2014. https://addicted2success.com/quotes/34-wayne-dyer-quotes-that-will-inspire -success-in-you.

Cameron, J. D., M. J. Cyr, and E. Doucet. "Increased Meal Frequency Does Not Promote Greater Weight Loss in Subjects Who Were Prescribed an 8-Week Equi-Energetic Energy-Restricted Diet." PubMed.gov. https://www.ncbi.nlm .nih.gov/pubmed/19943985.

"Common Food Allergy Triggers." WebMD. https://www.webmd.com/allergies/ food-triggers#1.

163

Corporation for National and Community Service, Office of Research and Policy Development. *The Health Benefits of Volunteering: A Review of Recent Research.* Washington, DC, 2007. https://www.nationalservice.gov/sites/default/files/documents/07_0506_hbr.pdf.

D'Adamo, Peter. *Eat Right for Your Type.* Berkley: 1996.

DeClerq, Katherine. "In Maya Angelou's Words: 'All Great Achievements Require Time.'" CTVNews.ca. May 28, 2014. https://www.ctvnews.ca/mobile/entertainment/in-maya-angelou-s-words-all-great-achievements-require-time-1.1842120.

Dr. Mercola. "Bromelain Can Help Abate Inflammation." Mercola: Take Control of Your Health. https://articles.mercola.com/vitamins-supplements/bromelain.aspx.

Dr. Mercola. "Here's What Eating Nothing but McDonalds for 10 Days Does to Your Gut Bacteria." Mercola: Take Control of your Health. May 27, 2015. https://articles.mercola.com/sites/articles/archive/2015/05/27/processed-foods-gut-microbes.aspx.

Editors of Rodale.com. "Top 12 Disease-Fighting Foods." *ABC Good Morning America.* https://abcnews.go.com/Health/Wellness/top-12-disease-fighting-foods/story?id=17886289.

Fletcher, Jenna. "Six Sciatica Stretches for Pain Relief." MedicalNewsToday, June 14, 2017. https://www.medicalnewstoday.com/articles/317920.php.

Frank, Monica A., and Susan Gustafson. "Exercise and the Self-Esteem Cycle." Excel at Life. https://www.excelatlife.com/articles/selfesteemexercise.htm.

Giovanni. "Master Your Mind, Master Your Life." Live and Dare. Last reviewed July 6, 2018. https://liveanddare.com/types-of-meditation.

Group, Edward. "The Health Benefits of Olive Oil." Global Healing Center. June 2014. https://www.globalhealingcenter.com/natural-health/benefits-of-olive-oil.

"Harmful, Fake Health Foods." Advanced Plan for Health. July 24, 2018. http://www.mypoindexter.com/index.cfm/news-events/blog/harmful-fake-health-foods.

Heitz, David, and Erica Cirino. "6 Stretches for Sciatica Pain Relief." Healthline. https://www.healthline.com/health/back-pain/sciatic-stretches.

Hofman, Wilhelm, Maike Luhmann, Rachel R. Fisher, Kathleen D. Vohs, and Roy F. Baumeister "Yes, But Are They Happy? Effects of Trait Self-Control on Affective Well-Being and Life Satisfaction," *Journal of Personality,* 82: 4 August 2014. https://onlinelibrary.wiley.com/doi/epdf/10.1111/jopy.12050?referrer_access_token=VYpCM2wGndCJqmYZilGMtYta6bR2k8jH0KrdpFOxC64ZkFBd IIHYLCNufdlB4xyAtl9yP9ZtcXvPx_xya63FhwmUKHtB-ODxLMBsZMS VQwxG-U2ASFxvMgPzK2V8H393

"The Importance of Matching Exercises to Your Body Type." Ufiit by Adrianne. https://ufiit.com/the-importance-of-matching-exercises-to-your-body-type.

Jimenez, Jesus. "10 Unforgettable Quotes." *Success Magazine.* September 2014. https://www.success.com/article/10-unforgettable-quotes-by-jim-rohn.

Jones, Sonia. "A Mindful Eating Meditation to Manage Food Cravings." *Yoga Journal.* January 26, 2015. https://www.yogajournal.com/lifestyle/mindful-eating-meditation-manage-food-cravings.

Justich, Kerry. "80-Year-Old Body Builder: 'Age is Nothing but a Number.'" Yahoo Lifestyle. June 20, 2016. https://www.yahoo.com/lifestyle/80-old-fitness-trainer -prove-000000042.html.

Kannall, Erica. "Role of Amylase." SFGATE. http://healthyeating.sfgate.com/role -amylase-8526.html.

Ladish, Lorraine C. "This Latina Bodybuilder Is 71: 'We Should Never Give Up on Ourselves.'" CBS News. July 24, 2017. https://www.nbcnews.com/news/latino/ latina-bodybuilder-71-we-should-never-give-ourselves-n786051.

LaFee, Scott. "Aging Casefully: 9 Things That Happen to Your Body (Some Aren't So Bad!)." *UC San Diego Health News.* August 2015.

Lewin, Evelyn. "How Preservatives Can Make Us Gain Weight." *Sydney Morning Herald.* August 19, 2017. https://www.smh.com.au/lifestyle/health-and-wellness/ how-preservatives-can-make-us-gain-weight-20170818-gxz28b.html.

"Lupus Facts and Statistics." National Resource Center on Lupus. 2018. https:// resources.lupus.org/entry/facts-and-statistics.

Manson, JoAnn, Eric Rimm, and Frank Hu. "Blood Type Linked to Heart Disease Risk." Harvard School of Public Health. August 14, 2012. https://www.hsph .harvard.edu/news/hsph-in-the-news/qi-blood-type-heart-disease-risk.

Marano, Hara Estroff. "Emotional Discipline." *Psychology Today.* June 9, 2016. https://www.psychologytoday.com/us/articles/200304/emotional-discipline.

Masicampo, E. J., and Roy Baumeister. "Consider It Done! Plan Making Can Eliminate the Cognitive Effects of Unfulfilled Goals." *Journal of Personality and Social Psychology,* June 20, 2011. doi:10.1037/a0024192.

Mayo Clinic Staff. "Food Allergy." Mayo Clinic. April 2, 2017. https://www.mayoclinic .org/diseases-conditions/food-allergy/symptoms-causes/syc-20355095.

Medaris Miller, Anna. "No Spouse, No Kids, No Caregiver: How to Prepare to Age Alone." *U.S. News & World Report.* October 26, 2015. https://health.usnews .com/health-news/health-wellness/articles/2015/10/26/no-spouse-no-kids-no -caregiver-how-to-prepare-to-age-alone.

"Meditation: In Depth." National Center for Complementary and Integrative Health. https://nccih.nih.gov/health/meditation/overview.htm.

Mindworks Team. "How Many People Meditate?" Mindworks. https://mindworks .org/meditation-knowledge/how-many-people-meditate.

Mindworks Team. "Meditation Definition: What Is Meditation?" Mindworks. https://mindworks.org/meditation-knowledge/meditation-definition-what-is -meditation.

Murray, Christopher J. L., Marie Ng, and Ali Mokdad. "The Vast Majority of American Adults Are Overweight or Obese, and Weight Is a Growing Problem among US Children." Institute for Health Metrics and Evaluation (IHME), http://www .healthdata.org/news-release/vast-majority-american-adults-are-overweight-or -obese-and-weight-growing-problem-among.

Nichols, Hannah. "What Happens to the Brain as We Age?" MedicalNewsToday. August 2017. https://www.medicalnewstoday.com/articles/319185.php.

"The 90+ Study." UCI Mind. http://www.mind.uci.edu/research-studies/90plus-study.

Nordqvist, Christian. Why Stress Happens and How to Manage It. MedicalNewsToday. November 28, 2017. https://www.medicalnewstoday.com/articles/145855.php.

"Osteoporosis and Asian American Women." National Institute of Arthritis and Musculoskeletal and Skin Diseases. https://www.bones.nih.gov/health-info/bone/osteoporosis/background/asian-american-women.

Palsdottir, Hrefna. "Does Junk Food Slow Down Your Metabolism?" Health-Line. March 21, 2017. https://www.healthline.com/nutrition/junk-food-and-metabolism#section2.

Pemberton, Corey. "7 Signs Your Gut Bacteria Are Out of Whack." Paleohacks. https://blog.paleohacks.com/7-signs-your-gut-bacteria-are-out-of-whack.

Price, Annie. "Lipase: The Digestive Enzyme that Fights Major Diseases. Dr. Axe. https://draxe.com/lipase.

Rock, David, and Josh Davis. "4 Steps to Having More 'Aha' Moments." *Harvard Business Review*, October 12, 2016. https://hbr.org/2016/10/4-steps-to-having-more-aha-moments.

Rogalski, Emily. "Cognitive Aging Summit III, Neurobiological Features of Super-Agers." https://www.youtube.com/watch?v=8_xu8uYMVEg.

Roman, Rodolfo. "Cancer Survivor Hopes to Complete Documentary about His Two-Time Fight with Disease." *Miami Herald*. November 16, 2015. https://www.miamiherald.com/living/health-fitness/article45118308.html.

Rutherford-Close, Amy. "7 Exercises to Improve Balance." Active. https://www.active.com/fitness/articles/7-exercises-to-improve-balance?page=2.

Ryback, Ralph. "Why We Resist Change." *Psychology Today*. January 25, 2017. https://www.psychologytoday.com/us/blog/the-truisms-wellness/201701/why-we-resist-change.

Santi, Jenny. "The Secret to Happiness Is Helping Others." *Time*. August 4, 2017. http://time.com/collection/guide-to-happiness/4070299/secret-to-happiness.

"Scientists Explain 'Aha!' Moments." WebMD. April 13, 2004. https://www.webmd.com/men/news/20040413/scientists-explain-aha-moments.

"The Secret to Better Health—Exercise." Harvard Health Publishing. https://www.health.harvard.edu/healthbeat/the-secret-to-better-health-exercise.

"7 Stretching & Strengthening Exercises for a Frozen Shoulder." Harvard Health Publishing. Updated November 29, 2017. https://www.health.harvard.edu/shoulders/stretching-exercises-frozen-shoulder.

Smith, Dana Leigh. "30 Worst Foods for Your Heart." Eat This, Not That. May 25, 2018. https://www.eatthis.com/foods-that-cause-heart-disease.

Snape, Joel. "Ectomorph, Endomorph and Mesomorph: How to Train for Your Body Type. Coach. September 1, 2017. http://www.coachmag.co.uk/lifestyle/4511/ectomorph-endomorph-or-mesomorph-what-is-your-body-type.

Sports Medicine. "What Your Body Shape Says about Your Health." UPMC. September 1, 2015. https://share.upmc.com/2015/09/what-body-shape-says-about-health-infographic.

Szalavitz, Maia. "Improving Willpower: How to Keep Self-Control from Flagging." *Time*. September 19, 2012. http://healthland.time.com/2012/09/19/improving-willpower-how-to-keep-self-control-from-flagging.

Waldinger, Robert. "What Makes a Good Life? Lessons from the Longest Study on Happiness." TED. https://www.ted.com/talks/robert_waldinger_what_makes_a _good_life_lessons_from_the_longest_study_on_happiness.

Walton, Alice G. "Different Types of Meditation Change Different Areas of the Brain, Study Finds." *Forbes*. October 5, 2017. https://www.forbes.com/sites/ alicegwalton/2017/10/05/different-types-of-meditation-change-the-brain-in -different-ways-study-finds/#e4168f61f1ea.

Ware, Bronnie. "Top 5 Regrets of The Dying." HuffPost. March 2, 2013, https:// www.huffingtonpost.com/bronnie-ware/top-5-regrets-of-the-dyin_b_1220965 .html.

"What Your Body Shape Says about Your Health." WebMD. https://www.webmd .com/diet/ss/slideshow-body-shape-health.

Williams, Mark E. "How Does Our Body Change as We Age? The Art and Science of Aging Well." *Psychology Today*. May 2017.

Yoga International. "What Are the 7 Chakras?" Yoga International. https://yoga international.com/article/view/what-are-the-7-chakras.

Index

abuse: aha moments and, 19; Domestic Violence Hotline for, 19; Liam emotional and verbal, 15

accountability, 48

action: aging and taking, 51, aha moments and, 2; defining moments and, 27; meal plan and, 75; purpose and, 130–32

addictions, 147

affirmations: Alexander on, 38; examples of, 38–39; for reclaiming health, 42–43, 44, 48; for rejoicing, 148

aging, 49; action and, 51; body building and, 50–51; daily checklist for gracefully, 55–56; menopause and, 50, 51, 52; questions on, 56; science of, 51–53, 54; super-agers, 53–54; superfoods and, 54–55, 56; well, 49

aha moments: abuse and, 19; action and, 2; clarity of mind, body, and spirit for, 21; defining moments and, 24–27; different, 21; experience-based, 23–24; how they work, 22–24; Janet having, 144; for Lashai, 25; lists and, 23; mindful meditation and, 22; purpose and, 131; resisting self-care and, 29; self-care questions and, 27–28; steps to having more, 22; why question and, 24

Aharon ("I don't deserve it" excuse), 37–38

Alexander, Ronald, 38

allergens, 65–66, 71; reactions to, 71 72; shellfish as, 72

American Dream, 9

Angela (rejoicing in life), 151

Angelou, Maya, 43

Anthony (meditater), 118–19

authority of your life. *See* becoming authority of your life

balance exercises, 90, 105

Bank Mobile, 123

Baumeister, Roy, 23

beauty. *See* deep beauty

Beck, Leslie, 79–81

becoming authority of your life: determination and, 10; discipline for, 11–12, 13; formula for, 8; goals for, 13; meanings of, 7; new thinking for, 12; plan into action for, 11; power and, 7, 12; questions for, 13

Ben (rejoicing in life), 150

Bernanos, George, 27

blood type: D'Adamo and, 67–68, 69, 70; diet for, 67–70, 77, 81, *82*; disease and, 64; finding out your, 70;

169

About the Author

Carolyn A. Brent is an award-winning and best-selling author and eldercare legislation advocate. She is also known as a body builder and health and wellness guru. She is the founder of Across All Ages and two nonprofit organizations, CareGiverStory Inc. and Grandpa's Dream. Her life mission is to help individuals and caregivers discover their own sense of personal strength in preparing for the future. Her research and extensive collection of published works have made her a notable figure in her field.

Carolyn received a BA in business administration from National University, in Los Angeles, and an MBA from the University of Phoenix in Pleasanton, California. Her professional background gives her rare insight into the complex medical issues facing people. For seventeen years, she worked for some of the world's leading pharmaceutical companies. As a clinical education manager for Pharmacia, she worked with key opinion leaders in the medical field. In her role as a senior therapeutic sales representative for another major pharmaceutical company, Novartis, she provided information to doctors and staff on a variety of subjects, including healthcare plans. Carolyn has also worked as a volunteer at various assisted-living facilities.

Carolyn's most impressive accomplishment has been her expansive body of work. The award-winning and best-selling *The Caregiver's Companion: Caring for Your Loved One Medically, Financially and Emotionally While Caring for Yourself* is in the Library of Congress, the libraries of Harvard, Stanford, and Johns Hopkins, and numerous other medical centers and universities. Designated as an Editor's Choice, she received the review of "excellent" by the *Library Journal*. Her other books include

- *Why Wait? The Baby Boomers' Guide to Preparing Emotionally, Financially and Legally for a Parent's Death*, a best seller on Amazon

- *The Caregiver's Legal Survival Guide: Navigating through the Legal System* (also available on audiobook and DVD)
- *The Caregiver's Financial Survival Guide: Navigating through the Financial System* (also available on audiobook and DVD)
- *The Caregiver's Emotional Survival Guide: Navigating through the Healthcare System* (also available on audiobook and DVD)

Carolyn is also the host of her own television show, *Across All Ages*, which airs on KHGI/KFXL in Nebraska.

She is the founder of Grandpa's Dream, a program that provides vital knowledge for the care and welfare of sick and disabled people and supports the mental, physical and emotional well-being of caregivers; and Caregiver-Story Inc., a nonprofit organization that provides free medical and legal resources to the public through a compelling website that attracts more than 300,000 visitors monthly. She is also a former member of the board of directors of Alzheimer's Services in the San Francisco Bay area.

Carolyn resides in Florida.